ACTORS ON SHAKESPEARE

A Midsummer N

F. MURRAY A

F. Murray Abraham   classical
and contemporary p   gn Beckett and
Pinter. He won an Aca   ms portrayal of Salieri
in Peter Shaffer's *Am*   He is a former Professor of
Theatre at City University of New York (Brooklyn). His dream
is to establish the British tradition of 'Panto' in America.

Colin Nicholson is the originator and editor of the Actors on
Shakespeare series published by Faber and Faber. He is the
author of the play *A Banquet of Crumbs*.

in the same series

F. MURRAY ABRAHAM

A Midsummer Night's Dream

Series Editor: Colin Nicholson

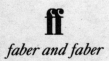

faber and faber

First published in 2005
by Faber and Faber Limited
3 Queen Square London WC1N 3AU

Typeset by Faber and Faber in Minion
Printed in England by Mackays of Chatham plc

A CIP record for this book
is available from the British Library

ISBN 0–571–21796–6

10 9 8 7 6 5 4 3 2 1

Introduction

Shakespeare: Playwright, Actor and Actors' Playwright

It is important to remember that William Shakespeare was an actor, and his understanding of the demands and rewards of acting helped him as a playwright to create roles of such richness and depth that actors in succeeding generations – even those with no reason or desire to call themselves 'classical' actors – have sought opportunities to perform them.

As the company dramatist, Shakespeare was writing under the pressure of producing scripts for almost immediate performance by his fellow players – the Lord Chamberlain's Men (later the King's Men), who, as a share-holding group, had a vested interest in their playhouse. Shakespeare was writing for a familiar set of actors: creating roles for particular players to interpret; and, being involved in a commercial enterprise, he was sensitive to the direct contact between player and audience and its power to bring in paying customers. His answer to the challenge produced a theatrical transformation: Shakespeare peopled the stage with highly credible personalities, men and women who were capable of change, and recognizable as participants in the human condition which their audience also shared. He connected two new and important elements: the idea of genuine individuality – the solitary, reflecting, self-communing soul, which is acutely aware of its own sufferings and desires; and, correlatively, the idea of inner life as something that not only exists but can also be explored. For him, the connection became the motor of dramatic action on the stage, as it is the motor of personal action in real life.

The primary importance of the actor cannot be disputed: it is his or her obligation – assisted to a greater or lesser extent by a director's overall vision of the play – to understand the personality they are representing onstage, and the nature of the frictions taking place when that personality interacts with other characters in the drama. Shakespeare's achievement goes far beyond the creation of memorable characters (Macbeth, Falstaff) to embrace the exposition of great relationships (Macbeth–Lady Macbeth; Falstaff–Prince Hal). Great roles require great actors, and there is no group of people in a better position to interpret those roles to *us* than the principal actors of *our* generation – inhabitants of a bloodline whose vigour resonates from the sixteenth century to the present day – who have immersed themselves in the details of Shakespeare's creations and have been party to their development through rehearsal and performance.

Watching Shakespeare can be an intimidating experience, especially for those who are not well versed in the text, or in the conventions of the Elizabethan stage. Many excellent books have been written for the academic market but our aim in this series is somewhat different. *Actors on Shakespeare* asks contemporary performers to choose a play of particular interest to them, push back any formal boundaries that may obstruct channels of free communication and give the modern audience a fresh, personal view. Naturally the focus for each performer is different – and these diverse volumes are anything but uniform in their approach to the task – but their common intention is, primarily, to look again at plays that some audiences may know well and others not at all, as well as providing an insight into the making of a performance.

Each volume works in its own right, without assuming an in-depth knowledge of the play, and uses substantial quotation to contextualize the principal points. The fresh approach of the many and varied writers will, we hope, enhance your enjoyment of Shakespeare's work.

Colin Nicholson
February 2002

Note: For reference, the text used here is the Arden Shakespeare.

Characters

Theseus, *Duke of Athens*
Hippolyta, *Queen of the Amazons, betrothed to Theseus*
Lysander, *a young courtier in love with Hermia*
Demetrius, *a young courtier in love with Hermia*
Hermia, *in love with Lysander*
Helena, *in love with Demetrius*
Egeus, *Hermia's father*
Philostrate, *Theseus's Master of the Revels*

Oberon, *King of the Fairies*
Titania, *Queen of the Fairies*
A Fairy, *in Titania's service*
Puck, *or Robin Goodfellow, Oberon's jester and lieutenant*
Peaseblossom, Cobweb, Moth, Mustardseed, *Fairies in Titania's service*

Peter Quince, *a carpenter; Prologue in the Interlude*
Nick Bottom, *a weaver; Pyramus in the Interlude*
Francis Flute, *a bellows-mender; Thisbe in the Interlude*
Tom Snout, *a tinker; Wall in the Interlude*
Snug, *a joiner; Lion in the Interlude*
Robin Starveling, *a tailor; Moonshine in the Interlude*

Other Fairies attending on Oberon and Titania
Lords and Attendants to Theseus and Hippolyta

A Midsummer Night's Dream was presented as the first play in Joseph Papp's Shakespeare Marathon at the New York Public Theater's Anspacher Auditorium from 7 December 1987 until 27 March 1988, with the following cast:

Theseus	Jack Ryland
Hippolyta	Patty Holly
Lysander	Rob Knepper
Demetrius	Bruce Norris
Hermia	Julia Gibson
Helena	Elizabeth McGovern
Egeus	Erick Avari
Oberon	Carl W. Lumbly/Joe Morton
Titania	Lorraine Toussaint
Puck	Geoffrey Owens/John Leguiziamo
Peaseblossom	Gwendolyn J. Shepherd
Cobweb	Torri Whitehead
Mustardseed	Sara Erde
Changeling	Mandla Msomi/Kennan Scott
Oberon's followers	David Calloway, Ron Dortch, Bryon Easley
Quince/Prologue	Richard Riehle
Bottom/Pyramus	F. Murray Abraham
Flute/Thisbe	Tim Perez
Snout/Wall	Joe Zaloom
Snug/Lion	Peter Appel
Starveling/Moonshine	Steve Hofvendahl

The production was set in Bahia, Brazil, c. 1900

This book is for Kate,
for Joseph Papp and Rosemarie Tischler,
and of course
for the Mechanicals

I would like to thank my editor, Colin Nicholson, for
pushing and pulling and shaping this book. It simply could
never have happened without him. Thank you, CGN,
Yr Obt. Serv., FMA

Foreword

I

'Let us raise a standard to which the wise and the honest can repair. The event is in the hand of God' – George Washington's words run along the cornice of the monument, where F. Murray Abraham and I stood at the end of an evening in New York. We met at one of his favourite restaurants to discuss writing a book based on his experience playing Bottom in Joseph Papp's production of *A Midsummer Night's Dream* for the New York Shakespeare Festival. After dinner Murray wanted to show me around Greenwich Village – his village – and we walked down Fifth Avenue to Washington Square. The Arch was cordoned off for filming, so we stood back and read the inscription.

From this spot, looking back up Fifth Avenue, you cannot help but feel moved by the spectacular sight of the buildings that illuminate the New York skyline, with the Empire State at its centre; but the opposite view, south across the Square, runs down West Broadway, and we looked toward the hole in the sky, on that particular evening full of light and dust rising from the clearing-work for 9/11. Murray is especially proud of his neighbourhood – he's not a native New Yorker but he loves New York, he loves being an actor and he loves Shakespeare.

It was through working with Murray that I understood the importance of Joseph Papp and the connection he was making between Papp and Shakespeare and actors – American actors. I was surprised by the amount of Shakespeare on offer – more productions listed in that week's *Village Voice* than in

London's *Time Out* – at the centre of which was Papp's New York Shakespeare Festival: free open-air performances at the Delacorte in Central Park during the summer and repertory all year at The Public.

Joseph Papp asked many questions about the relevance of Shakespeare: 'Why do so many thousands of people get hooked on Shakespeare and develop a habit that lasts a lifetime? What can he really say to us today, in a world filled with inventions and problems he could never have imagined? And how do you get past his special language and difficult sentence structure to understand him?' Actors are in the ideal position to answer such questions, for they inhabit the characters and speak to us with true feeling. Maybe that's why I love actors so much: these words can remind us of the better men we wish to be, the stronger hearts we want to have and the generosity of spirit to enlighten and please our fellow man. Shakespeare wrote such words.

Joseph Papp spoke enthusiastically for Shakespeare: 'You might not know much about Shakespeare, or much about the theater, but when you watch actors performing one of his plays on the stage, it will soon become clear to you why people get so excited about a playwright who lived hundreds of years ago. For the story – what's happening in the play – is the most accessible part of Shakespeare.' Murray acknowledges Papp as crucial in any assessment of Shakespeare, acting, and modern theatre and makes full use of the play's thematic line 'The course of true love never did run smooth' throughout his book. This clearly resonates with Papp's summary of the way Shakespeare's plays touch all of us – 'In *A Midsummer Night's Dream*, for example, you can immediately understand the situation: a girl is chasing a guy who's chasing a girl who's chasing another guy. No wonder *A Midsummer Night's Dream* is one of the most popular of Shakespeare's plays: it's about one of the world's most popular pastimes – falling in love.'

On 7 December 1987 *A Midsummer Night's Dream* kicked off Joseph Papp's complete cycle of plays for the New York Shakespeare Festival; he cast big-name actors, persuading stars to take part for under $400 per week. Sadly he did not live to see its completion – when the final play in the marathon was performed in 1993, he'd been dead for three years – but he saw Murray play Bottom.

Murray is an advocate for Shakespeare 'with an American accent'. I latched on to the seeds of his argument during the read-through of *Richard III* in Al Pacino's documentary, *Looking for Richard*: 'The problem with being an American in Shakespeare is you approach it reverentially, we shouldn't but we do, and we have a feeling, I think, of inferiority to the way it has been done by the British.' Papp's desire was to cast an exclusively American Shakespeare.

Murray's honesty as an actor extends beyond his craft to his behaviour as a man – in fact I can't separate the two. A journeyman actor for the first half of his career, his life was changed by being cast as Salieri in *Amadeus*, but even the starring role in a huge film did not dazzle or deflect him and his focus and integrity remain intact. He was reading for a small part in *Amadeus* when director Milos Forman asked him to help by taking the part of Salieri with a young actor auditioning for Mozart. Milos was so impressed that he called him and said he was his 'first choice for the part', but Murray wasn't overly enticed. 'I've been around for a while, you know, so I said, "Well that's nice, I'm very happy about it, but what does that mean?"; see, he wasn't saying, "You've got the part," or "I really want you to do it and there's no question about it" – he said, "You're my first choice." Now, from my point of view that doesn't pay the rent. I'm very flattered – thank you, Milos – but just tell me what I have to do next because I'm very busy right now painting my kitchen!'

'Been around for a while' meant many things – New York stage: Broadway, Shakespeare; television: *Kojak*; films: *Serpico*, *Scarface* – but it also made him who he is as an actor and his career incorporates everything the hardworking actor doing good work will face. Bottom is this actor: enthusiastic, brave and champion of his Mechanicals. Bottom's triumphs are unselfconscious. He does not see the difficulties and walks through life with boundless self-confidence; he is equal to any situation, and uses a more ambitious vocabulary than he can master. This is Bottom's way, preparing for dreams of stardom.

On the street in his crumpled white linen suit with his shirt unbuttoned to his waist, Murray wasn't quite strutting but he was certainly commanding – old-timers walking their dogs waved, ladies smiled, drivers honked, kids on bikes shouted. In the restaurant the maître d' cleared the most prestigious table (that would have comfortably held ten) for the two of us – everybody noticed him, it was a procession. As we ended the evening at the base of the Washington Arch we anticipated with excitement the book you now hold.

II

Just a glance at the reviews shows how much Murray's performance at the Anspacher Theater was appreciated by the critics:

> Abraham is a born stage-taker, his unselfconscious ego an endless source of warmth and energy. And Bottom is a role in which ego is not only allowable but mandatory, Abraham rocks the audience just by letting Bottom's huge complacent smile shine out. – *Village Voice*

> The acting has a fine naturalistic bent to it and a special comic gusto that would not come easy to British Shakespeareans. Prominent here is F. Murray Abraham's

Bottom . . . Abraham, very smart to stress the animalistic aspect of Bottom . . . extremely charming and wonderfully endearing in his showbiz conceits. – Clive Barnes

Striking performance delivered by F. Murray Abraham as Bottom – by design the hammiest and most conceited of amateur actors. Antoon's transplantation of the play works most smoothly with Bottom and his fellow Mechanicals . . . with or without his ass's head, he is clownishly in character and remains so even after his pro-longed death scene in the play within the play. Miming deadness, he reflexively regains the spotlight by reaching for his sword and placing it within the grasp of the grief-stricken Thisbe in order to encourage him to conclude his own extended death scene . . . As is often the case with Shakespeare, the most persuasive acting transcends any directorial overlay. The performances by Ms McGovern and Mr Abraham, in particular, could be lifted out of con-text and would work with equal efficiency in a divergent setting. – Mel Gussow, *New York Times*

One has the feeling of witnessing a great classic interpre-tation while F. Murray Abraham has a field day as Bottom. – *Atlanta Journal*

III

In the 1920s and 30s Harley Granville-Barker was commis-sioned to write introductions for a new edition of Shake-speare's plays, but the publisher abandoned the project when it proved too costly. Granville-Barker's extant essays number fourteen. The Actors on Shakespeare series numbers ten. The objective was not to mirror Harley Granville-Barker's 'Prefaces to Shakespeare', but to build upon Granville-

Barker's initiative for actors to write about the plays: 'They might profit more written a generation hence, for the ground they build upon is still far from clear. And this introduction is by no means a conspectus of the subject; that can only come as a sequel' – and actors truly are the possessors of a tradition, the proud inheritors of Shakespeare.

Joseph Papp said: 'Shakespeare's a symbol of the theater, a symbol of certain standards, of values in life. There's something very affirmative about it. It is, you know, deep – governments come and go, wars come and go, and there Shakespeare is . . . I learned everything I know about the theatre through Shakespeare. And it was always a source of wonder.'

There is a certain symmetry that F. Murray Abraham's *A Midsummer Night's Dream* should be the 'finale' volume in our Actors on Shakespeare series, as it was the inaugural production in Joseph Papp's American cycle.

> Our revels now are ended. These our actors,
> As I foretold you, were all spirits, and
> Are melted into air, into thin air:
> And, like the baseless fabric of this vision,
> The cloud-capp'd towers, the gorgeous palaces,
> The solemn temples, the great globe itself,
> Yea, all which it inherit, shall dissolve,
> And, like this insubstantial pageant faded,
> Leave not a rack behind. We are such stuff
> As dreams are made on; and our little life
> Is rounded with a sleep.
>
> [Prospero, *The Tempest*, Act IV, scene i]

Colin Nicholson
June 2004

PART I

View from the Bottom

An Elizabethan context

The center of the universe continues to shift. For a long time it was the earth. Then it became the sun. Now there is no center at all, just billions of tiny particles speeding through us, ignoring us, not even bothering to shoulder us aside while they visit the thousands of parallel worlds that overlap and surround us. Giordano Bruno described something like this to the court of Queen Elizabeth in his 'Theory of Concentric Worlds', and I wonder if that partly inspired Shakespeare's concept of the fairies in *A Midsummer Night's Dream*.

The fairy world is certainly an ancient fantasy, and in literature it usually takes a metaphoric leap in the dark to get there: you jump in a lake; step through a wardrobe (to Narnia) or into a hole in a wall; and to 'be' John Malkovich find Floor $7^1/2$ and enter his portal – but whatever it is, you need to travel into a separate world to get there. In Shakespeare's vision it is right here, truly parallel to our own world, accessible by a walk into the woods. Its citizens inhabit an alternative space living side by side with us. And though visits from the fairies are common enough, a visit to their world is hard to pull off; a guide is needed, an interpreter who is able to communicate easily with the inhabitants of this bizarre otherworld and link them for us convincingly to the everyday world of Athens.

To make that communication plausible, Shakespeare had to create someone with a substantial ego, someone who could recognize the existence of many other egos, but subdue them sufficiently by the sheer size of his own generous, charming, overwhelming confidence – someone who would believe himself to be the center of any universe; in other words, an actor.

Bottom

Of course, an actor. After all, inventing worlds is our stock in trade and apparently it's a healthy thing to do. In America, actors have one of the lowest rates of suicide – psychiatrists one of the highest. This puzzles me, as both professions deal with basically the same thing: understanding and making whole another human being. Maybe psychiatrists should be required to take acting classes. Maybe everyone should. You find out amazing things about yourself by pretending to be someone else, and Bottom, the character I played, is a natural – ostensibly a weaver, he dramatizes every moment of his life. He is Shakespeare's great character actor and consequently to analyze Bottom is to analyze acting.

What a feast is this role, a one-man banquet. Bottom's claim, 'I can play taller, shorter, fat, thin, I can do it,' is the actor's credo, for unless an actor believes himself capable of this ability to interpret everything and nothing, he'll soon establish limitations and become complacent. Shakespeare gives Bottom his cue to carry the torch for every actor who has asked just for the chance to 'show his stuff'. Like any good actor, he's ready to find out everything about himself. I love his confidence, his exuberance, his desire to be involved in every single thing. His openness is disarming and invites us to respond in kind. He accepts so completely who he is (and who he can be), that we are almost forced by his healthy self-regard to acknowledge its justification, and even if we feel skeptical of his persistent optimism, we also feel slightly envious of it. There is a wonderful irony in how I've described Bottom because it is completely opposite to the way I was feeling when Bottom was offered to me in autumn 1988.

Frankie and Johnny in the Claire de Lune

I had just come through a desperately bitter experience concerning the original theatrical production of Terrence McNally's *Frankie and Johnny in the Claire de Lune*. Terrence was a dear, old friend – we met in 1972 when I auditioned for his off-Broadway play *Where Has Tommy Flowers Gone?* – and over several years I performed or read publicly every play he wrote: *Bad Habits*, *Ravenswood*, *The Ritz* (later made into a film directed by Richard Lester), *It's Only A Play*, *Lisbon Traviata*, and eventually *Frankie and Johnny in the Claire de Lune*. He knew my work well and had written the play as a two-hander for me and Kathy Bates (if not specifically, then with us both very much in mind) and we were crucial to Terrence's conception of the characters and therefore crucial in the overall formation of the play as a workshop production. There is a special Equity contract that allows union actors to work for almost nothing (below scale rates) in order to try out new plays, giving opportunities to experiment and develop work – equally good for writers and performers: it encourages and helps fledgling plays that might not otherwise find an audience and/or investors. A maximum of four weeks rehearsal and two weeks of performance is permissible, with the understanding (promise) of the role to the actor in the event of a full production. My personal history with the play went back even further (about a year), involving public readings and discussions of early drafts. With the remarkable Ms Bates as Frankie, we became very, very good together. It was her first naked scene, although not her last, as she appeared nude with Jack Nicholson in the hot-tub scene for

3

About Schmidt (2002). What terrific company Kathy keeps for disrobing herself.

My association with Terrence had explored a variety of roles, so he knew me well, and with *Frankie and Johnny in the Claire de Lune* I thought he had written something spectacular for me, opposite an actress I adored, in a perfectly tailored modern play. So for those two weeks, in an auditorium the size of a postage stamp, about nine hundred people saw the best work I had ever done. In other words, it was a dream come true. And that was the last time I did it. I had been contracted to shoot a film overlapping the play's schedule (for the transfer of the full production) by two weeks, and the producers were either unwilling or unable to change the dates. If you want to get an actor's blood up, ask him to tell you about 'the one that got away' – we all have stories of losing a job through schedule conflicts. It's possible to go for months without work, forcing you to take the first thing that comes along, only to be offered a plum the day after you sign. But if you can stick around long enough, things even out; into your lap falls somebody else's loss. In some cases, as in this one, losing a job can be a blessing.

When the off-Broadway production finally became a reality it did so without its original Johnny. The loss to me was devastating and it awakened all of those 'actor's doubts' that I thought I'd finally laid to rest with the arrival of 'Oscar'. The Academy Award for Best Actor in *Amadeus* changed my life. Instead of auditioning, I was inundated with offers, but what crap so many of those offers were. Salieri was much rarer than I had realized. Peter Shaffer's creation was brilliantly originated by Paul Scofield at the National Theatre in London; Ian McKellen won the Tony in New York; and for me it won the Oscar. Obviously, Peter is largely responsible for our success, but great contemporary roles don't come along very often and

Johnny was like a ray of sunshine for me. When I lost it I lost my bearings.

I realize now that I wanted to do *Johnny* for all the wrong reasons – to change my image, to show off what I could do in a custom-made part. One value in doing it was good business sense, and more than a touch of vanity – I really looked good without clothes. I guess it's plain that I was being swept up in the 'biz' of show business. Now the doubts came flooding back, and there is nothing worse than doubt for an actor – or a lover, for that matter. I truly was 'rescued' by *A Midsummer Night's Dream*.

Leaving the theater

My plight was so like that of the misguided lovers in *A Midsummer Night's Dream* – their longing was mine, their need, their passion and fury were mine too, and . . . their sadness. I was so much in love with this bitch of a theater and she didn't seem to give a damn about me. I wanted nothing more to do with her and was ready to pull up stakes and go to Los Angeles and work for mammon. Hell, I thought, if my heart is going to be broken, let it be for money. Then along came *A Midsummer Night's Dream*, for $350 a week.

'The course of true love never did run smooth' couldn't be a more accurate description of my dilemma. There I am, planning my divorce from the theater, when impresario Joseph Papp appears and invites me to be part of a spectacular project. The presentation of all thirty-six of Shakespeare's plays, six a year for six years, launching his program with *A Midsummer Night's Dream*.

Joseph Papp

Of course I immediately rejected it. What else could I do? I

5

had my pride, and I'd already sworn to devote my life to television, where the money is, but ... but Shakespeare ... with Joseph Papp ... Now, that's an event. Joe's presentation of Shakespeare was like throwing down a gauntlet. He challenged us to do it American-style, and if we didn't know what that was, he insisted we make it our business to find out. What he didn't want was a carbon copy of the British, which is how Americans usually do Shakespeare. Understandably so: most of our models for performance have been British, many of our teachers use British recordings as guides, and critics generally seem to prefer the British interpretations. This is less a complaint than an observation.

Like Joseph Papp was, I am a vigorous crusader for Shakespeare with an American accent. There is some conjecture that English as spoken in certain isolated Appalachian communities approximates Elizabethan pronunciation, which might make an interesting American *Macbeth* (the myths of the Hatfields and McCoys); but all that aside, I don't think any actor can give an honest performance of anything while impersonating someone else. If Shakespeare is as universal as everyone says, then let his words be spoken the way I speak. There's a joke among New York actors:

'What's the difference between good acting and great acting?'

'What?'

'An English accent!'

That joke would be funny, except for the way it affects otherwise good actors. They become weird around Shakespeare, their bodies stiffen, their voices change, and they start to sing their lines. American actors are especially guilty of this and there is no need for them to be. Al Pacino has made great strides toward helping Americans eliminate that self-consciousness, along with Christopher Walken, whose classical roles outnumber those by any other prominent American actor. But it was Joseph Papp who was the torchbearer. He had been hacking away at it for years.

New York Public Theater

Joseph Papp was the most prolific, innovative theatrical producer in America. He produced plays, directed plays, published a quarterly anthology of new plays, presented Shakespeare off portable stages in poor sections of town, and he did what no one dreamed possible: he built the Delacorte, a permanent/temporary theatre in New York City's sacrosanct Central Park, in order to present free 'Shakespeare in the Park' for anyone who wanted to come. He also reclaimed the huge Astor Place Library, a 113-year-old brick structure in lower Manhattan (with the help of the New York Landmarks Commission, and in 1971 sold it to the city for $2.6 million with a deal to lease it back for $1 a year!) and made it the headquarters for the New York Public Theater and Shakespeare Festival, reviving that entire moribund area of Manhattan. The Public Theater auditorium was subsequently renamed, in his memory, the Joseph Papp Public Theater. He converted it into a complex of offices, rehearsal spaces, a cinema, and six theatres. *A Chorus Line* originated there, as did *Hair*, among hundreds of other productions (he even put together a one-man musical evening starring himself) and now *A Midsummer Night's Dream*. According to the *New York Times*, Joseph Papp was obviously my model for Bottom, but only now do I realize how true that was and proudly recognize the unconscious tribute.

He cared so much and knew so much about Shakespeare – in vivid, personal terms – his eyes would sparkle when he talked about him. His declared goal was to introduce

Shakespeare to Americans on their own terms and therefore the first step in breaking down barriers was to give the audience productions in which performers with familiar diction were speaking with American accents. Traditional casting went out the window and the critical establishment went into a tizzy, but they hadn't counted on Joe's response. He was a street fighter and always went to the wall for his people. I worked for him on several experimental projects that got some of the worst reviews I've ever read, some that were so bad I had to laugh. But Joseph Papp didn't laugh. He'd be there at the next performance to tell us the critics were out of their minds, and further, that he had called each of them to tell them the same. He was completely devoted to the idea of a truly 'public' theater, with American Shakespeare at its center.

I should add that my loyalty and high regard for him was long in coming. I auditioned for the New York Shakespeare Festival for almost seven years before they hired me, so when I pay these compliments to Joe, they are not idle niceties. Those were a long seven years, and bitter. He has earned his praise and remains the man I most admire in the American theater. All of which is by way of explaining that it was only a matter of time – twenty-four hours – before I called his executive producer, Rosemarie Tischler, and asked if it was too late to be Bottom. She said they had been expecting my call. This production dragged me out of my depression and into the best theatrical experience of my life. Re-reading *A Midsummer Night's Dream* was a wake-up call.

The commission: a wedding

It's revealing that *A Midsummer Night's Dream* was not written primarily for the commercial theatre. There is some speculation that it was an entertainment for a private wedding, which must have contributed to its playfulness and joy. Can you imagine the discussion with Shakespeare about the commission? 'Will, I want you to come up with a fun play for my wedding. There'll be about three hundred people, so we better do it outside under the trees. There are going to be some children, so you should include something for them. Oh, and the Queen might drop by.' In case you're thinking of doing the same for your own wedding, you should know that the groom in this case happened to be the patron of Shakespeare's theater company.

There is no record of the first performance, but perhaps it took place in the mid-1590s, at the wedding of the granddaughter of Henry Carey, who was the patron of the Chamberlain's Men – Shakespeare's company – or possibly at the wedding of the Earl of Derby. Derby's older brother, Lord Strange, had been the company's patron before his death in 1594.

Weddings are sexy – fancy clothes, wine, music and dancing – love is in the air, and bawdy jokes are in order; and to me the well-lubricated guests at a wedding reception sound like a great audience. It might be that writing an entertainment for that giggly, rowdy, happy celebration, rather than the box office, is what encouraged Shakespeare and gave him the freedom to create one of his few original plays. *A Midsummer Night's Dream* is relatively unusual in not having a readily identifiable main source – although the play within the play, 'Pyramus and Thisbe' (the Interlude), is from Ovid's *Metamorphoses*. There are various sources for the characters and some of the situations are also identifiable, but the story is his invention. It is a little intricate, yet no matter how complex the relationships, we have no trouble following the action. It toys with our imagination, both delighting and troubling us, like a dream verging on nightmare, which is probably the way many people feel shortly before their wedding day.

Separation of the worlds

Three worlds are represented in the play: two by the dual social structure of the everyday world (upper class and artisans), alongside the mystical world of the fairy folk. The common element is love, and its vicissitudes, and the event that unites these separate societies is the wedding of Theseus and Hippolyta, announced at the beginning of the play, that finally takes place in the last act when it is augmented by the betrothal of the two pairs of young lovers. As entertainment for the nuptial celebration, six workers or artisans rehearse a 'tragic' play that one of them has written, 'Pyramus and Thisbe'. The Interlude contrasts doomed poetic love with the aristocratic version we've witnessed through the course of the drama, but it also heightens a further comparison with the magical, dangerous love of the feuding King and Queen of the Fairies (Oberon and Titania), who have come to bless the ceremony.

Bottom is the only Athenian character connecting the three worlds, and the extent to which he achieves success in this endeavor is measured by how well he involves the audience in his make-believe world through his portrayal of his unusual experiences. When Coleridge's 'willing suspension of disbelief' is misquoted, by dropping 'willing', it is a serious omission, as it undermines the necessary complicity of the audience. They *wish* to be fooled. They *will* themselves to believe that what they are looking at is true, but it lasts only from one moment to the next. In exchange for their belief, they demand a similar commitment from the performer – the audience expects the actor to convince them that what is being said is true. They have to believe that Bottom is certain of his abilities, capable of instantly rising to any occasion with ease and style, otherwise they won't accept the idea that he fits so readily into the arboreal enchanted world.

PART II

Act I, scene i

'I woo'd thee with my sword'

Theseus, Duke of Athens, has conquered the Amazonian Queen, Hippolyta. He then falls for her and plans to marry her in a few days. I wonder about the warrior Hippolyta's true feelings for this guy who strides into her kingdom, whips her army, then arranges to marry her – I think he'd better sleep with one eye open. In the opening lines of the play Theseus muses that four days is a long time to wait to consummate the marriage, but the Amazon puts him off; even the great hero Theseus can't take love for granted.

THESEUS
    Now, fair Hippolyta, our nuptial hour
    Draws on apace; four happy days bring in
    Another moon: but O, methinks, how slow
    This old moon wanes! She lingers my desires,
    Like to a step-dame or a dowager
    Long withering out a young man's revenue.

HIPPOLYTA
    Four days will quickly steep themselves in night;
    Four nights will quickly dream away the time . . .

Theseus is aware of the harm he has caused to Hippolyta but attempts to reconcile her by saying he will wed her in 'another key' and calls on his Master of Revels, Philostrate, to arrange celebrations for the wedding – hoping no doubt that this will assuage any thoughts of vengeance on her part and demonstrate his respect by elevating her to be his Queen.

13

Diplomacy was an emerging strategy for the expansionist Elizabethan power and the contradictory behaviour of Theseus would therefore have been better understood by Shakespeare's English audience than we might imagine.

THESEUS

Go, Philostrate,
Stir up the Athenian youth to merriments;
Awake the pert and nimble spirit of mirth;
Turn melancholy forth to funerals;
The pale companion is not for our pomp.
    Exit Philostrate.
Hippolyta, I woo'd thee with my sword,
And won thy love doing thee injuries;
But I will wed thee in another key,
With pomp, with triumph, and with revelling.

His sweet love plans are interrupted by sour Egeus, who drags in his daughter Hermia, and her two suitors Lysander and Demetrius. Hermia loves Lysander, but her father insists that she marry Demetrius. Judging from this opening scene, Athens is a harsh place to live if you're a woman.

EGEUS

Full of vexation come I . . .
As she is mine, I may dispose of her;
Which shall be either to this gentleman,
Or to her death, according to our law . . .

THESEUS

What say you, Hermia? Be advis'd, fair maid.
To you your father should be as a god:
One that compos'd your beauties, yea, and one
To whom you are but as a form in wax
By him imprinted, and within his power

14

To leave the figure, or disfigure it.
Demetrius is a worthy gentleman.
[...]

HERMIA

... But I beseech your Grace that I may know
The worst that may befall me in this case,
If I refuse to wed Demetrius.

THESEUS

Either to die the death, or to abjure
For ever the society of men.
Therefore, fair Hermia, question your desires,
Know of your youth, examine well your blood,
Whether, if you yield not to your father's choice,
You can endure the livery of a nun ...

Theseus declares that Hermia must agree to marry Demetrius
or choose between death and a convent (and all that implies).
No one questions why Egeus would prefer to see his daughter
dead than not married to Demetrius. And what about
Demetrius? Has he considered what it might be like being
married to someone who loves another? Of course we realize
that alliances and political strategies were entwined in the
marriage contract, especially for the nobility, but this hard-
ened attitude to one's own daughter is harsh and difficult to
understand. Does it not occur to Demetrius that it might be
best to quit the field, or is it his nature only to pursue? As we
find out later, he has similarly pursued Hermia's friend
Helena, the woman who now loves and pursues him, and he
has rejected her. Is Demetrius a repressed, latent homosexual,
in love with Lysander and hoping to punish him by denying
Hermia to him? Or is he simply a bored, spoilt rich kid in a
male-dominated society with laws and customs that favor
him and his whimsical nature?

Young love

In the opening scenes of Act I Shakespeare establishes very quickly the strict sense of order, progression and law in Athens, which is set in contrast to the anarchy of the forest. The wild forest is where most of the action in the play takes place, and where anything goes. Shakespeare introduces this other place, this fantasy world, as an environment where all these mortal conflicts and situations can be resolved.

Left alone with Hermia, the wildly passionate Lysander speaks the famous line that colors the whole evening (at least in our production), 'The course of true love never did run smooth,' and Hermia's response legitimizes their love by suggesting it is the great test of all true loves:

HERMIA
    If then true lovers have been ever cross'd,
    It stands as an edict in destiny.
    Then let us teach our trial patience,
    Because it is a customary cross,
    As due to love as thoughts and dreams and sighs,
    Wishes and tears, poor fancy's followers.

Young lovers

A solution presented by Lysander is for them to go to his aunt's house, so Hermia and Lysander decide to escape Athens, and agree to meet in the woods the next night in order to elope to said aunt's demesne. By introducing the 'widow aunt' Shakespeare unwittingly previews the pantomime aspects in the role of the spinster and the comic possibilities associated with it: mistaken identity, the chase, thwarted love, etc.

Helena enters, mournfully yearning for Demetrius, who

now despises her, having at one time wooed her. Hermia confides to Helena their plan to escape from Athens and Helena decides to tell Demetrius about the rendezvous in the woods, as she plans to accompany him there in his pursuit of Hermia in hope to win his attentions.

Elizabeth McGovern played Helena, gaining the respect of all who remembered how she had been savaged by the press in *The Two Gentlemen of Verona*. She came to the play with a calm determination, and, at the same time, a lightness appropriate to Helena. She showed no nerves, no doubt whatever. As a veteran recipient of critical whippings for certain performances, I know how hard it is to get back out there. This lovely actress never hesitated or doubted herself and from the first reading it was evident that this was going to be a fine piece of work.

This same wood, where the two pairs of young lovers have arranged to meet, is also where we are introduced to the Fairy Kingdom – an alternative society, one that contrasts with Athens but also offers freedom, the sort of escapist freedom only offered beyond a boundary. These woods are dangerous, and all who enter are in peril; even the Fairy Queen herself doesn't go to sleep without a spell being cast to protect her. Danger is an important element, as is moonlight, and they are connected.

Everything about our director's concept and staging of *A Midsummer Night's Dream* was full of ambivalence: moonlight, the drums, the jungle, the Fairies, all both romantic and fearful. And danger was not only in the wild jungle, but in highly civilized Athens as well. The decision to escape to this wild kingdom is fearsome and thrilling, but much more than that, it is the magical glade where happiness and joy are a reality; it serves as another Eden, a blessed world where miracles can happen.

Act I, scene ii

The Mechanicals

Theseus's call for revels has led to a competition amongst the townspeople to perform an Interlude at the wedding feast. This gives the play another dimension by introducing the underclass, represented here by one of Shakespeare's great inventions of repertory theatre – the Mechanicals. These six artisans have names that reflect their occupations: Peter Quince, from 'quines' or 'quoins' (wooden wedges a carpenter used); Nick Bottom, a weaver, the bottom being the reel on which a skein of thread or wool was wound; Tom Snout, a tinker who repairs the spouts or snouts of kettles; Francis Flute, for the fluted sides of organs or bellows that he fixes, and the high voice he uses later as Thisbe; Robin Starveling, a tailor, a profession of proverbially thin men; and Snug, the joiner, a furniture maker whose name refers to close-fitting joints.

Peter Appel, who played Snug the joiner, is a big but graceful man, a collegiate hockey player of immense strength and gentleness. He was the Lion in the Interlude, but I like to think of him as Baloo the bear, from Kipling's *Jungle Book*. Like Baloo, he is a counselor to persons in distress, which he does gratis. The Lion's speech in 'Pyramus and Thisbe' (Act V, scene i) sounded as though it had been written for Peter – so suitable he was ready to perform the role immediately – but, never satisfied, he continually worked on it. The company had a core of actors who worked out every night before the show, and Peter was one. We would each go through the trouble spots in our performances privately, quietly mumbling lines to ourselves, weaving around each other on that small stage as we practiced new moves and gestures. It must have looked like a scene from *Marat-Sade*. Within a month most of the actors were satisfied, but Peter continued to experiment, and about once a week he'd ask me to take a look at something he'd come up with.

Steve Hofvendahl – Robin Starveling the tailor – is meditative and thoughtful. His large blue eyes quietly observe, only seldom blinking. Yet he doesn't stare. Rather, he gazes and digests at the same time. His reflective nature proved ideal for this character, who plays the part of Moonshine (the moonlight). His costume was the trickiest one. He carried a long fishing pole, with a lantern on the end of it to represent the moon. In an effort to raise the moon that much higher, he walked on six-inch platform shoes, one shoe with a tiny dog on it, the other with a thorn bush. The stage set was partially on a steep incline and in those shoes Steve had to negotiate that ramp very carefully. Instead of treating it as a problem, Steve converted his careful steps into a majestic journey of the moon in the sky.

As The Mechanicals come together to cast 'Pyramus and Thisbe', the play written by Quince, we made our first entrance loudly singing and dancing a samba version of 'The Woozel Cock', borrowed from Bottom's song in Act III, scene i.

QUINCE Here is the scroll of every man's name which is
    thought fit through all Athens to play in our interlude
    before the Duke and the Duchess, on his wedding-day at
    night.

It is immediately clear that Peter Quince, like any writer showing his work for the first time, is nervous; 'his wedding day at night' always got a laugh – a surprised gasp of a laugh – because Richard Riehle read it so subtly they weren't sure they had heard correctly. But Bottom has no such reservations and his forthright exchanges with the writer/director, Quince, establish Bottom as the central figure – the star.

BOTTOM First, good Peter Quince, say what the play treats on; then read the names of the actors; and so grow to a point.
QUINCE Marry, our play is 'The most lamentable comedy, and most cruel death of Pyramus and Thisbe'.
BOTTOM A very good piece of work, I assure you, and a merry. Now, good Peter Quince, call forth your actors by the scroll. Masters, spread yourselves.

And so Bottom is the first to be cast – as Pyramus – and once he has asked, 'What is Pyramus? A lover, or a tyrant?', he then proceeds to describe how well he will act it as a lover but that his real talent is for a tyrant, which he proves with some epic poetry:

BOTTOM That will ask some tears in the true performing of it. If I do it, let the audience look to their eyes: I will move storms, I will condole in some measure. To the rest – yet my chief humour is for a tyrant. I could play Ercles rarely, or a part to tear a cat in, to make all split.
>   The raging rocks,
>   And shivering shocks,
>   Shall break the locks
>   Of prison-gates;
>   And Phibbus' car
>   Shall shine from far
>   And make and mar
>   The foolish fates.
This was lofty. Now name the rest of the players . . .

Bottom thinks a lot of himself and does not hesitate to say so – is he being boundlessly enthusiastic or taken over by his character? This is unquestionably an actor talking, a particular type of actor, and apparently we haven't changed much since the Elizabethan period. As soon as he hits the stage he is in charge – he starts to manage the rehearsal of the new play, gets the leading role, speaks eight lines of tragic poetry from memory, auditions for two other roles, does some directing, and has the last word in the scene, all in less than fifty lines. This requires a bravura performance of a size and energy that may surprise even the actor himself.

Still unsatisfied, Bottom wants to be cast as several other characters in addition to Pyramus: '. . . let me play Thisbe too. I'll speak in monstrous little voice . . .' But Quince insists: 'No, no, you must play Pyramus . . .'

When Bottom performs the role of the young maiden, he must not play a silly party game; it must be sincere. This performance should be in the great tradition of British pantomime, where cross-dressing is fun and camp but also truthful. In other words, he must be very good at what he does, even when he's ridiculous – especially when he's ridiculous: 'Let me play the lion too. I will roar, that I will do any man's heart good to hear me . . .' and when he does it, he really has to ROAR.

But Quince placates him: 'And you should do it too terribly, you would fright the Duchess and the ladies, that they would shriek: and that were enough to hang us all.'

During one particular matinee, in our very intimate theatre, a nine-year-old girl in the second row burst into tears when Bottom roared like a lion, so I went to her and explained that it was all make-believe, that there was nothing to be afraid of; and eventually I convinced her and her birthday party to roar with me. It was a little hard to get them to quiet down again, but what fun it was, and how in keeping with the play.

This next exchange between director and actor could be happening at this very moment in theatres anywhere in the world:

QUINCE You can play no part but Pyramus: [pause] for
    Pyramus is a sweet-faced man; [pause] a proper man as
    one shall see in a summer's day; [pause] a most lovely,
    gentleman-like man: [pause] therefore you must needs
    play Pyramus.
BOTTOM Well, I will undertake it.

Each of the colons and semi-colons in Quince's speech is a pause, because Bottom is moping for being rebuffed by Quince. Bottom's feelings have been hurt, and he must be soothed before the rehearsal can continue. Shakespeare's knowledge of actors and acting really pays dividends here. Bottom must be wooed, because without him there is nothing. Quince is admirable in his manipulation; which is genuine flattery, as opposed to false flattery. One of the keys to portraying the Mechanicals is sincerity and the actors playing them must not be condescending to these characters. We look to them for equilibrium; it would be easy to play them as individuals and by so doing overlook their cohesive and vital nature as a group of actors working collectively in a repertory company, and one of the great strengths of our production was unity. In order for both the fantastical fairy people and the vacuous young nobility to float untethered, they need the Mechanicals to function as anchors to reality.

The Mechanicals decide to rehearse privately in the woods the next night and before they depart Bottom has to have the last word:

BOTTOM We will meet, and there we may rehearse most
    obscenely and courageously. Take pains, be perfect: adieu!

QUINCE At the Duke's oak we meet.
BOTTOM Enough: hold, or cut bow-strings.

Act II, scene i

The enchanted woods

The second Act opens with this change of location and introduces us to the Fairy World – just a walk away into the woods
of Athens – already noted as the place where Lysander has
arranged to meet Hermia, and also the place where the
Mechanicals have arranged to rehearse.

The woodland is a mysterious, magical environment –
reflected in the scenery – and we suggested its variance with
the everyday (Athenian) world by using elements from the
Americas. The inhabitants of our Fairy World were distin-
guished by their ethnicity and color, with origins in Africa,
Puerto Rico, the Caribbean, Cuba and Mexico – often
marginalized communities in the United States. This conceit
portrayed the Fairies as magical gods and elves from the
South American jungle, where magic is still a living, natural
part of the culture. In the latter part of the twentieth century
the English-speaking world got hip to Magical Realism and in
a palatably diluted form it became a fashionable cultural
characteristic of South America. To underscore the ambience
of this other world, improvised music was always playing in
the woodland scenes, whether gently percussive or more
aggressively stomping (especially for the dancers), its presence forming a kind of soundtrack.

Puck and the Fairy enter the woods to rapid drumming,
and drums continue as a subtle undercurrent until their exit,
which is precipitated by the arrival of Oberon and Titania,

whom they see approaching from separate directions. Puck and the Fairy depart to avoid the inevitable squabbles of this couple, whose arguing they have been discussing.

'Ill met by moonlight'

Puck (Robin Goodfellow) and the Fairy speak of the argument between their master (Oberon) and mistress (Titania) but also outline their own inclinations to mischievousness. They say the King and Queen of the Fairies are avoiding one another because Titania refuses to hand over an Indian changeling boy and Oberon wants her to give him up to him. It looks to me like arguments are an integral part of their domestic dialogue: they accuse one another of over-familiarity with Theseus and Hippolyta. As if that isn't enough, Titania suggests that their arguing has affected the climate and confused the seasons. She sees it as no joke; already it has spilt over and caused damage to the entire countryside through intolerable, unseasonable weather. Shakespeare used recent destructive weather conditions in England to pull his audience into the reality of his Fairy Kingdom by showing the disruptive power of nature.

With the arrival of Oberon and Titania we've now encountered all the pairs of lovers and outlined their respective troubles. Shakespeare extends this theme of lovers' dilemmas to incorporate Peter Quince's 'Pyramus and Thisbe' (in which the lovers die), as a counterpoint and also a kind of foretelling of *Romeo and Juliet,* which Shakespeare wrote during this lyrical period of his career that also produced *A Midsummer Night's Dream.* The Interlude ends in death for Thisbe and Pyramus, but the other couples – Theseus/Hippolyta, Hermia/Lysander, Demetrius/Helena – move toward a happy resolution with their multiple betrothals. 'The course of true love never did run smooth.'

Do not discount the Fairy Folk as purely a fantasy element: they are to be reckoned with, and their blessing on Duke Theseus's nuptial day is very important in that superstitious time – much like now, in certain parts of America, also (but quite differently) in India, where the eunuchs are traditionally required to bless a wedding as a lucky symbol of the celebration.

Oberon and Titania

OBERON
Ill met by moonlight, proud Titania.

TITANIA
What, jealous Oberon? Fairies, skip hence;
I have forsworn his bed and company.

OBERON
Tarry, rash wanton; am not I thy lord?

TITANIA
Then I must be thy lady . . .

In her line, 'Then I must be thy lady,' Titania admits the bond of fealty to her lord, but what she wants, and what she does, is to remind him of his fling with Hippolyta, 'the bouncing Amazon, / Your buskin'd mistress and your warrior love,' to illustrate one reason for not doing his bidding; and Oberon responds with gossip involving her and Theseus:

How canst thou thus, for shame, Titania,
Glance at my credit with Hippolyta,
Knowing I know thy love to Theseus?
Dids't not thou lead him through the glimmering night . . .

This banter complicates, and adds some spice, by layering our understanding of the opening scene between the Duke and the Amazon Queen. Oberon insists that Titania give him a particular changeling boy as his henchman; it is never clear why, especially after Titania's beautiful, touching speech describing how much the boy means to her.

OBERON

Why should Titania cross her Oberon?
I do but beg a little changeling boy
To be my henchman.

TITANIA

Set your heart at rest:
The fairy land buys not the child of me.
His mother was a votress of my order;
And in the spiced Indian air, by night,
Full often hath she gossip'd by my side;
And sat with me on Neptune's yellow sands,
Marking the embarked traders on the flood:
When we have laugh'd to see the sails conceive
And grow big-bellied with the wanton wind . . .
But she, being mortal, of that boy did die;
And for her sake do I rear up her boy;
And for her sake I will not part with him.
[. . .]

OBERON

Give me that boy, and I will go with thee.

TITANIA

Not for thy fairy kingdom. Fairies, away!
We shall chide downright if I longer stay.
Exit Titania and her Train.

Despite his great power, and later his sensitivity to the young lovers, in this one instance Oberon, like Egeus, seems an obdurate, small-minded man, with no regard for anything but his own selfish desires. Or was this just a test to demonstrate his power and her subservience? Was this partly an elaborate lesson for *his* woman – a reminder to her, and to all women, of their place in life?

If so, it didn't make much of a dent in our strong ladies. They played their refusals to the men with gusto and force, as though the independent woman was demanding her love be earned through respect.

Oberon sets out to punish his Queen. He sends his servant Puck to fetch a magic flower and squeeze its juice into Titania's eyes while she sleeps:

OBERON

Fetch me that flower; the herb I show'd thee once.
The juice of it, on sleeping eyelids laid,
Will make or man or woman madly dote
Upon the next live creature that it sees …

PUCK

I'll put a girdle round about the earth
In forty minutes.
    Exit.

OBERON

Having once this juice,
I'll watch Titania when she is asleep,
And drop the liquor of it in her eyes:
The next thing then she waking looks upon,
(Be it on lion, bear, or wolf, or bull,
On meddling monkey, or on busy ape)
She shall pursue it with the soul of love.

'I am invisible'

Demetrius enters a clearing in the woods with Helena in pursuit. Oberon eavesdrops on them and demonstrates the extent to which Magic is an effective force and plays upon reality in this mysterious world by making himself invisible; he simply says, 'I am invisible.' One of my favorite lines in the play, it makes me feel like a child, and I want to shout, 'I am too, I am too.'

Helena, deeply in love with Demetrius, continues to entreat him; he rejects her, leaves, and she follows. Oberon, registering Demetrius's disdain for Helena, determines to help her and punish Demetrius for rebuking the smitten young lover. When Puck returns, Oberon tells him to put some of the flower's juice on the eyelids of the man wearing Athenian clothing.

Act II, scene ii

Titania is sung to sleep by her retinue, then left alone. Oberon appears with the magic flower and squeezes some of its juice onto her eyelids.

OBERON

> What thou seest when thou dost wake,
> Do it for thy true love take;
> Love and languish for his sake.
> Be it ounce, or cat, or bear,
> Pard, or boar with bristled hair,
> In thy eye that shall appear
> When thou wak'st, it is thy dear.
> Wake when some vile thing is near.
>   *Exit.*

At this point Oberon had another little magic trick, igniting some *flash paper* (which is an explosive, usually harmless, stage effect); he could give the impression of creating fire. One particular night, when Oberon did this trick, a flaming piece of the flash paper leapt up into Joe Morton's (Oberon's) hair, but he wasn't to know of the unexpected burst of flame on his head. Since the only other actor onstage with him at the time was the sleeping Titania, Lorraine Toussaint was oblivious to the unintentional drama and Joe continued the scene unaware that his hair was on fire.

The auditorium we were working in was not a conventional proscenium theatre but a converted library with the stage on the same level as the audience, the seating climbing at a steep angle with the control booth behind. The stage manager could see what was happening, but couldn't get to Joe and his smoldering hair. He was about to make an announcement on the public-address system when a woman in the first row of seats stepped onto the stage and smothered the flame with her scarf. She whispered to him what had happened, returned to her seat and Joe finished his speech. At the end of the performance, he brought the lady onto the stage for a curtain call.

Lysander and Hermia find a place to lie down and sleep, but Hermia insists that they maintain a respectful distance from each other. Puck (sent by Oberon to seek the man in Athenian clothing), finds the couple sleeping far apart, assumes that they must be the Athenians he is supposed to help fall in love and squeezes some juice on Lysander's eyes. His task complete, Puck exits.

Helena and Demetrius enter. He flatly rejects her pleas, and again leaves her. Helena is distraught and shows so much of the emotion that young girls in love must go through – the deep insecurities, worries of attraction, comparisons to her friend, (in this case) the beautiful Hermia.

HELENA

O, I am out of breath in this fond chase!
The more my prayer, the lesser is my grace.
Happy is Hermia, wheresoe'er she lies,

For she hath blessed and attractive eyes.
How came her eyes so bright? Not with salt tears;
If so, my eyes are oftener wash'd than hers.
No, no; I am as ugly as a bear,
For beasts that meet me run away for fear:
Therefore no marvel though Demetrius
Do, as a monster, fly my presence thus.
What wicked and dissembling glass of mine
Made me compare with Hermia's sphery eyne?
But who is here? Lysander, on the ground?
Dead, or asleep? I see no blood, no wound.
Lysander, if you live, good sir, awake!

LYSANDER [*Waking*]

And run through fire I will for thy sweet sake!
Transparent Helena! Nature shows art,
That through thy bosom makes me see thy heart.
Where is Demetrius?

Helena wakes Lysander, and under the spell of the juice he falls in love with her. Lysander's immediate declaration of love (under the spell – of course!) for Helena shows how fickle men can be, but also illustrates his/their fears, by quickly asking (with some concern) about the whereabouts of Demetrius, his rival. Helena is shocked by his behavior and spurns this declaration – first, for the infidelity toward Hermia, but also because she thinks Lysander mocks her. She exits. Lysander, in a reverse of roles, follows in pursuit of Helena. Hermia awakens from a nightmare and finds herself alone.

Although all scenes require equal care to design and stage (suitable to adapt easily to variations in theatres) these scenes of mismatched couples required the kind of careful planning that supports and almost drives the narrative. The co-ordination must be convincing or the audience has a tendency to get distracted and lose interest if it doesn't flow effectively. You mustn't see the technicalities of staging; they must subtly permeate the text unnoticed.

The sets were necessarily minimal, as the stage had been converted from what had been, I think, the Rare Book section in the Astor Library complex. It's a tight space, with a thrust stage surrounded on three sides, nearly no wing space, and two columns right and left of center. Entrances were made through either of two vomitories in the audience, or above right and left of the columns. The back wall had an exit door, which by law had to remain uncovered throughout the performance, and occupied the most prominent position on the stage – up center – so we sometimes made a show of making 'an exit'. The sets were simple flats cut in the shape of jungle plants, that rolled quickly on and off. The columns served well for Athens, with an elegant throne as the single set piece in the first act. For the 'masque' at the end, the Mechanicals supplied their own 'set', a few pieces that we wore or carried with us. Quince's house was two flats, one with a door and the other with a window, that rolled on from opposite ends of the stage. (That house trapped an unsuspecting Mechanical one evening, coming in so fast that he was wedged between two sets; he worked his way to the window and spoke his lines from there.) The only place to put the musicians was above the audience, floating on a steel platform, suspended from the ceiling. The lighting was one of the most important elements in the setting of each scene. That may sound trite, but in a play that is supposed to take place by the light of a sliver of a moon, the balance between believability and being seen becomes critical. It worked well, thanks to the brilliance of the designers: scenic design, Andrew Jackness; lighting, Peter Kaczorowski; and costumes, Frank Krenz.

Act III, scene i

'Are we all met?'

BOTTOM There are things in this comedy of Pyramus and
Thisbe that will never please. First, Pyramus must draw a
sword to kill himself; which the ladies cannot abide. How
answer you that?

The Mechanicals come to a suitable place in the woods for
their planned rehearsal, and unbeknownst to them Titania is
up above, asleep in the treetops. Through force of personality
Bottom immediately takes charge of the rehearsal and starts to
drive the scene.

BOTTOM Not a whit; I have a device to make all well. Write
me a prologue, and let the prologue seem to say we will do
no harm with our swords, and that Pyramus is not killed
indeed; and for the more better assurance, tell them that I,
Pyramus, am not Pyramus, but Bottom the weaver. This
will put them out of fear.

This scene could be happening right now in any number of
television or film productions. Bottom is the star, without
whom there is no show, and the star's comments are always
'for the good of the production', which usually means more
material for himself. Invariably during nineteenth-century
Shakespeare productions, the star performer (and company
leader) could do any great speech, or crowd-pleasing turn, no
matter what character he was playing. For instance, Edwin
Booth was expected to change out of his Brutus costume to
deliver Mark Antony's 'Friends, Romans, countrymen' speech.
Bottom is not Booth, but his instinct for the limelight is sec-

ond to none. His ability to capture center stage extends beyond this group of friends to every scene he is part of, and he is not overawed by the Fairies, nor is he cowed by the great Duke Theseus. He simply dominates each world he encounters. The harm that he may inflict is to Quince's script, when, like so many producers today, he wants to meddle. It's funny to think that Bottom feels so superior to the upper class, having as little regard for the intellectual capacity of the aristocracy as most filmmakers have for the bourgeoisie, the media and critics. The essential difference is Bottom's absence of cynicism. He's like the kid who, when he gets tossed into a room full of horse manure, starts to dig excitedly, shouting, 'There's got to be a pony in here somewhere.'

BOTTOM Nay, you must name his name, and half his face must be seen through the lion's neck; and he himself must speak through, saying thus, or to the same defect: 'Ladies,' or 'Fair ladies, I would wish you,' or 'I would request you,' or 'I would entreat you, not to fear, not to tremble: my life for yours! If you think I come hither as a lion, it were pity of my life. No, I am no such thing; I am a man, as other men are': and there, indeed, let him name his name, and tell them plainly he is Snug the joiner.

Is Bottom asserting the power of drama, or the whims of a precious and overly self-conscious actor? Look at the tendency in Hollywood to compromise a script through focus groups so as not to offend any potential audience. This sensitivity deflates the dramatic power of the original work by making it palatable to the lowest common denominator. This kind of simplification reaches a level of ridicule with the inclusion of Wall and Moonshine, although it is, I suppose, possible to see them in an opposite light of being fantastic surreal creations.

BOTTOM Some man or other must present Wall; and let him
   have some plaster, or some loam, or some rough-cast
   about him, to signify wall; and let him hold his fingers
   thus, and through that cranny shall Pyramus and Thisbe
   whisper.

The Mechanicals' rehearsal of 'Pyramus and Thisbe' is
incorporated by Michael Powell and Emeric Pressburger as
part of an important scene in their World War II surreal love
story, *A Matter of Life and Death*, whereby British and
American servicemen are rehearsing the play as an entertainment, which comments on the difference in approach to
Shakespeare of American and English actors, and I will
address the contrasting styles later in my text.
   Puck has stumbled upon this gathering close by his Queen,
and while observing Bottom's behavior, Puck thinks this man
is an idiot, a bit of an ass, and as a joke decides to play a trick
on him. When Bottom, for all this preciousness, suggests that
Pyramus and Thisbe do not die; that the Lion is only the joiner dressed up, etc., Puck decides to make mischief:

PUCK
   What hempen homespuns have we swaggering here,
   So near the cradle of the Fairy Queen?
   What, a play toward? I'll be an auditor;
   An actor too perhaps, if I see cause.

Mischievously Puck decides to turn Bottom's head into that
of an ass at the moment in the Interlude rehearsal when
Flute/Thisbe says, '*As true as truest horse that yet would never
tire*'. Bottom re-enters with the words, '*If I were fair, Thisbe, I
were only thine*,' unaware of the transformation that has overcome him; but when his friends see this witchcraft, they run
away with Puck at their heels. The idea of Puck having a crew

of silent helpers to join him in scaring the wits out of the Mechanicals adds an element of terror to this scene, a genuine sense of pandemonium on being abandoned in the woods.

Bottom cannot understand why he has been left all alone in the dark, sings to bolster his courage and awakens sleeping Titania.

BOTTOM [*Sings.*]
    The ousel cock, so black of hue,
    With orange-tawny bill,
    The throstle, with his note so true,
    The wren with little quill –
      [*The singing awakens Titania.*]

TITANIA
What angel wakes me from my flowery bed?

BOTTOM [*Sings.*]
    The finch, the sparrow, and the lark,
    The plain-song cuckoo gray,
    Whose note full many a man doth mark,
    And dares not answer nay –

For this I did a limbo dance to 'The Woozel Song', and as Titania's flowery tree-bed descended from the heavens, I bent backwards lower and lower until I was on the floor, and she settled right in my lap, as sexy an entrance as a character man could ask for. It was also a wonderful piece of staging to show her waking to my song and, under the spell of Oberon's making, falling in love with the first living creature that she looks upon.

I promise you, when I put on that ass's head, I felt instantly potent, randy, and very, very attractive. You should try it sometime with your sweetheart. It doesn't have to be an ass's head particularly, just any old beast that appeals. You both might be in for a big surprise. The best thing about this metamorphosis for me, though, was the way it affected the rest of my performance.

No matter what anyone else did or thought, I was going to be the paramour of a panting, lovesick, beautiful queen – and all that that implies: ego, self-confidence, arrogance; reason goes out the window. Hey! I'm a Love God! I know that before the curtain goes up, an actor should not think about what is going to happen later in the play, and that he should concentrate on 'the now'. But . . . give me a break – you see, I have never been selected one of the 'Sexiest Men in the World', and that's how Lorraine Toussaint (Titania) made me feel: 'Thou art as wise as thou art beautiful'!

'I do love thee: therefore go with me'

Titania declares her passion for Bottom. She entreats him to stay and does her best to persuade him that she will make it worth his while:

> And I do love thee: therefore go with me.
> I'll give thee fairies to attend on thee;
> And they shall fetch thee jewels from the deep,
> And sing, while thou on pressed flowers dost sleep:
> And I will purge thy mortal grossness so,
> That thou shalt like an airy spirit go.
> Peaseblossom! Cobweb! Moth! And Mustardseed!

Here is one of the moments in the play which I so looked forward to, when she cooed this beautiful poetry for me:

TITANIA
> Come, wait upon him; lead him to my bower.
> The moon, methinks, looks with a watery eye,
> And when she weeps, weeps every little flower,
> Lamenting some enforced chastity.

I ripped off my shirt with a huge 'HEEE HAAAAWWW', put my arm through her legs and lifted her straight up in the air. We danced off the stage that way, with her balanced on my protruding arm and holding on to my ass's head, with the retinue of fairies dancing around us to sinuous drums. Best of all, I had nothing to fear from King Oberon. Extraordinarily this love affair with Bottom only amuses Oberon. Whereas she has twice accused Oberon of jealousy, he cannot be jealous of a weaver disguised as an ass.

The aspect of an animal famous for its giant penis violating one's wife is a serious contemplation for all three characters, but especially for the violator, when you consider the husband has nearly unlimited power. After the event Oberon makes no mention of the incident, and as he and Titania are reconciled, he probably feels satisfaction by showing his power over her. Is it possible that Bottom is at least part of the reason that Oberon is so equable? Oberon knows this is only happening because he arranged it – so why should he feel threatened? If you had to arrange for your wife to be seduced, for whatever reason, with whom would you be least angry? Why, Bottom of course. He's so feckless and charming, you can't be jealous of him. Life is so seductive that he can't resist any invitation it presents, taking each opportunity, but never with malice.

Act III, scene ii

'This falls out better than I could devise'

Puck tells a delighted Oberon of Titania's love for the transformed Bottom and immediately he wants to know if Puck completed his instructions to manipulate the other couple.

OBERON

   This falls out better than I could devise.
   But hast thou yet latch'd the Athenian's eyes
   With the love-juice as I did bid thee do?

Puck assures him that this task has been undertaken.

   Then Hermia and Demetrius enter and Oberon observes
their frantic dialogue – Hermia questions Demetrius of the
whereabouts of Lysander and argues that he would not aban-
don her, concluding that Demetrius must have killed him. She
stomps off, and Demetrius, tired out, goes to sleep. Witnessing
this exchange, Oberon realizes that Puck has charmed the
wrong Athenian and, to set this situation right, instructs him
to bring Helena to them, while he squeezes the love-juice onto
the eyes of the sleeping Demetrius.

   Helena enters, followed by a lovesick Lysander. Demetrius
wakes up, sees Helena, and he too falls in love with her. She is
now confused by this change in her fortunes and angrily
accuses Lysander and Demetrius of toying with her. Hermia
appears, looking for Lysander, and once she has found him is
puzzled at his newly professed love for Helena; Helena, in
turn, takes that as a mocking insult; she concludes that
Hermia, Lysander and Demetrius are ganging up on her,
taunting her. There is almost a fistfight among the four of
them. 'The course of true love never did run smooth.'

   But now some sadness comes to underpin this farce.
Hermia and Helena have been the closest of friends since
childhood, and if you look more closely at some of their
exchanges in this scene, hurtful and painful, you will see them
as not a little prophetic of the rivalries love can bring to all
women, however close in friendship.

HELENA

   Injurious Hermia! Most ungrateful maid!

Have you conspir'd, have you with these contriv'd,
To bait me with this foul derision?
Is all the counsel that we two have shar'd,
The sisters' vows, the hours that we have spent
When we have chid the hasty-footed time
For parting us – O, is all forgot?
All school-days' friendship, childhood innocence?
We, Hermia, like two artificial gods,
Have with our needles created both one flower,
Both on one sampler, sitting on one cushion,
Both warbling of one song, both in one key,
As if our hands, our sides, voices and minds,
Had been incorporate. So we grew together,
Like to a double cherry, seeming parted,
But yet an union in partition,
Two lovely berries moulded on one stem;
So, with two seeming bodies, but one heart;
Two of the first, like coats in heraldry,
Due but to one, and crowned with one crest.
And will you rent our ancient love asunder
To join with men in scorning your poor friend?
It is not friendly, 'tis not maidenly;
Our sex, as well as I, may chide you for it,
Though I alone do feel the injury.

HERMIA

I am amazed at your passionate words:
I scorn you not; it seems that you scorn me.
[...]
                    ... she hath made compare
Between our statures; she hath urg'd her height;
And with her personage, her tall personage,
Her height, forsooth, she hath prevail'd with him.
And are you grown so high in his esteem

39

Because I am so dwarfish and so low?
How low am I, thou painted maypole? Speak:
How low am I? I am not yet so low
But that my nails can reach unto thine eyes.
[...]

HELENA
O, when she is angry, she is keen and shrewd;
She was a vixen when she went to school,
And though she be but little, she is fierce.
[...]
                    I will not trust you, I,
Nor longer stay in your curst company.
Your hands than mine are quicker for a fray:
My legs are longer though, to run away.
    Exit.

HERMIA
I am amaz'd, and know not what to say.

Although the text makes plain the difference in height
between Hermia and Helena, and obviously the casting
reflected this physical difference, our Hermia, Julia Gibson,
was not intimidated by Elizabeth McGovern, who towered
over her. She used the physical disadvantage to introduce
techniques to help her character convey aspects of herself. She
had the habit of pushing up her sleeves when Hermia became
angry, as though about to do battle, a wonderfully funny ges-
ture in light of the twelve-inch difference in height.

The women are now at odds with each other, and so are the
men. Lysander and Demetrius charge off to have a duel.
Helena runs from Hermia's wrath, and Hermia, confused,
exits.

Oberon resolves to correct this negligence that Puck has
caused. He sends Puck to make a fog to first safely separate the

two men so that they don't duel, and by using voices to distract them from one another removes the charm from Lysander's eyes. Puck tricks the men into chasing around harmlessly through the fog he creates, until they collapse and sleep. Helena and Hermia, also exhausted, find places nearby to sleep. Puck squeezes the love-juice on to Lysander's eyes, and ends the scene with a gentle song of reconciliation, which becomes the theme for the next scene.

PUCK

> On the ground
> Sleep sound;
> I'll apply
> To your eye,
> Gentle lover, remedy.

Squeezes the juice on Lysander's eyelids.

> When thou wak'st,
> Thou tak'st
> True delight
> In the sight
> Of thy former lady's eye;
> And the country proverb known,
> That every man should take his own,
> In your waking shall be shown:
> Jack shall have Jill
> Naught shall go ill;
> The man shall have his mare again, and all shall be well.

Act IV, scene i

Like a soundtrack signifies a mood, the gentle music that accompanies Puck's speech fills the wood with peace and grace, creating an atmosphere of calmness, which is sustained into the following scene and quite typical of the way instruments were used in our production. The musicians were granted considerable freedom to contribute to the performance, and this additional element of improvisation lifted and changed the performance each night. They gave themselves over to the play – supporting, leading, soloing – so supple and flexible, so characteristic of the sensuous nature of South American music and rhythms. The barehanded drums and keyboards were complemented and the percussive effect was deepened by the bare feet of the dancers and at times the real possibility of magic, a beneficent, positive magic, filled the theater.

When Lorraine as Titania declared her passion for me as Bottom, I had to remind myself that it wasn't me she had the hots for – she was only acting. But it was terrific to let myself believe, for a brief time, I was her one and only, because that's the impression she gave. I think this is one of the reasons actors and actresses are resented by some people who have probably been on the receiving end of the initial burst of charm that thespians are capable of, only to discover that others get the same treatment. People who are not familiar with actors take that 'rush of affection' very personally, when in fact it is not so much phony as a natural response to a new acquaintance. This is not true of all actors – some of us are aloof and surly – but when we turn on the charm it can be very convincing.

I fell victim to the charms of Judy Davis in a film we did together in Australia. In *Children of the Revolution* she plays a character who is desperately in love with Stalin (me), and has traveled halfway around the world to meet him. In our crucial emotional scene she is dressed in an evening gown and enters Stalin's private dining room through a set of double doors, and the first thing she sees when the doors open is me. Even as an Old Pro, I simply wasn't prepared for what happened; she looked at me and literally took my breath away. I knew this woman loved me to distraction, and I felt myself swelling up – I couldn't accept that she was acting. No. Obviously she had fallen head-over-heels in love with me, not with the character – WITH ME. It's flattering to be loved, even if it's acting, and most of us are susceptible.

'Come sit thee down upon this flowery bed'

Titania and Bottom (with his ass's head) arrive in a woodland clearing where Lysander, Demetrius, Helena and Hermia are still sleeping. They are attended by the Fairies, and Oberon has followed them (unseen).

TITANIA

> Come sit thee down upon this flowery bed,
> While I thy amiable cheeks do coy,
> And stick musk-roses in thy sleek smooth head,
> And kiss thy fair large ears, my gentle joy.

It doesn't get much better than this! In every way Bottom is indulged by the attendant Fairies, but I played it as though Bottom has just petered out – when we stumbled back onstage, I needed help from all sides, and the last thing on my mind was more dalliance; so when Titania asks him, 'Or say, sweet love, what thou desir'st to eat?', my first thought was: 'Oh no, not again.' Bottom replies, 'I could munch your good dry oats. Methinks I have a great desire to a bottle of hay: good hay, sweet hay,' then starts looking for a place to lie down with the line, 'good hay, sweet hay, hath no fellow'. Titania responds with some downright bawdy lines:

> I have a venturous fairy that shall seek

The squirrel's hoard, and fetch thee new nuts.
[...]
Sleep thou, and I will wind thee in my arms.
Fairies, be gone, and be all ways away.

Exeunt Fairies.

So doth the woodbine the sweet honeysuckle
Gently entwist; the female ivy so
Enrings the barky fingers of the elm.
O how I love thee! How I dote on thee!

They sleep.

Bottom is tired and wanting of sleep, as Titania strokes him and fondles him. She sends the Fairies away, takes him in her arms, and so entwined, they fall asleep.

Oberon has been watching and tells Puck, 'Her dotage now I do begin to pity . . .', because Titania is at a disadvantage – 'I then did ask of her her changeling child; / Which straight she gave me . . .' He has manipulated Titania and now feels sorry, or even ashamed:

. . . I will undo
This hateful imperfection of her eyes.
And gentle Puck, take this transformed scalp
From off the head of this Athenian swain.

And as Titania wakes she remembers something of a dream she had, but is glad to see Oberon: 'My Oberon! What sweet visions have I seen! / Methought I was enamour'd of an ass.'

Under the instruction of Oberon, Puck has tied up all the loose ends – Oberon is reconciled with his Queen, and the audience pretty much knows the end is near. Puck removes the ass-head from Bottom, and the Fairies cause music that will put the lovers and Bottom into a deeper sleep. Then they go off to prepare a dance of blessing for the wedding ceremony.

Theseus, Hippolyta and Egeus (and their train) have entered the woods and stumble upon the young lovers while hunting with hounds. The lovers wake to the sound of the horns (music is everywhere in this play), whilst in the meantime they have been restored, not only to themselves but also to each other. They attempt to explain, to the newly arrived Athenians, what has been happening. Lysander admits his plan to elope with Hermia and Egeus demands Lysander's execution for trying to stop Hermia marrying Demetrius. Demetrius declares his love for Helena. Theseus overrules Egeus, declaring that Hermia may marry Lysander. Theseus then commands that both sets of couples – Lysander/Hermia and Demetrius/Helena – should also be married that day at the forthcoming ceremony of his own betrothal to Hippolyta. 'The course of true love never did run smooth.'

Bottom's Dream

Theseus and the hunting party leave for Athens, and the lovers talk about the dreamy state they are in, and when they too depart for Athens, Bottom is left alone in the woods. As Bottom wakes, he has a similar experience to Titania and the young lovers, in that he is awestruck by his recollection of experiences and thinks it must have been a dream. He tries to hang on to the dream and runs off to share it with his fellow artisans.

So I'm alone on stage – abandoned – at a pivotal moment in the play. Bottom thinks it was a dream and is inspired to use it for his upcoming performance in the Interlude, anxious to meet again with his fellow dramatists. This quiet moment before the big finale is a fine piece of theatrical engineering by Shakespeare; he creates it in order to let us take a breath, and also to separate ourselves from the Fairy World – the stillness

45

allows us to settle back. Bottom is uncharacteristically reflective at the beginning of the short speech that concludes the scene, but by the end of it he should be completely awake and propelling the play back to reality, carrying the audience with him. It is an important moment for Bottom and the actor can take his sweet time, but must not allow the audience to get ahead of him. In it Shakespeare presents the loveliest opportunity to the actor. It's as though he were standing there, paging the curtain back and gesturing the actor toward the stage:

BOTTOM . . . I have had a most rare vision. I have had a dream, past the wit of man to say what dream it was. Man is but an ass if he go about to expound this dream. Methought I was – there is no man can tell what. Methought I was – and methought I had – but man is but a patched fool if he will offer to say what methought I had.

This is how it went for me.

While the audience is absorbed watching Titania and Oberon make up to one another and as the other parties return to the status quo, Bottom remains onstage, but he has to be restored to being the weaver (without the mask), transformed in time for the start of the monologue. I took the opportunity to sneak off the ass's head so that it seemed to have magically disappeared when Puck suddenly snapped his fingers and gestured toward me. As I described earlier, I liked that head and liked what it did for me a lot, so I truly missed it when it was gone, which added a great deal of credibility to Bottom's speaking of pleasurable memories.

Sore spot

The ass's head took several hours of sitting while a mold was made of my head and neck, after which two more visits to the mask-maker were necessary for adjustments. His design was based on a caricature of my features and fitted me very well, although there was one problem: I developed an allergic reaction to the material. I mistakenly thought it was simply an abrasion and applied some cream to the sore spots, but it became more and more irritated until my neck and shoulders were swollen and raw. This was during rehearsals and worsened considerably as we approached opening night.

The show was flying together – actors, musicians, dancers, costumes, technicians – so there was very little time to pay a hell of a lot of attention to my rash. I continued to apply salves and creams while the management promised to bring in the designer as soon as he was available. This went on until we'd been playing to preview audiences for about a week. New York theater is a small world and the show was a big hit long before the critics came. We were all enjoying the success so much that I feared my unsightly, swollen neck was never going to be taken care of unless I did something drastic, so after a performance I stopped A. J. Antoon in the crowded lobby of the theater, peeled off my shirt and showed him my miserable, blotchy problem. You have to understand, this is a director I loved dearly, one of the very best I have ever worked with (rest his soul), but the show was 'up', as far as A J was concerned, his job was done. That's a reasonable assumption, considering the months of preparation he'd gone through, and his attitude was: 'Why should *I* have to deal with FMA's complaint?' A J said something to that effect and told me to take it up with the management, and with increasingly loud voices we turned our conversation into a shouting match.

I said, I'd like *him* to do something about it.

He responded, that he wasn't a doctor.

So I told him, that if it wasn't taken care of by tomorrow –

instead of wearing the mask, I would appear with a printed sign on my forehead that read 'jackass'.

To which he replied, 'If you do, you won't go on.'

I yelled, 'Oh yeah? Then who's gonna do the part?'

And he rose up to his full five feet eight inches and screamed: 'I AM!'

We both started laughing hysterically. The crowds in the lobby must have thought it was part of the show, because it was so in keeping with the fun of the entire evening. The next day a simple piece of moleskin was added to the inside of the mask, solving the problem in five minutes.

Other actors who've played Bottom yield nightmare stories about ill-fitting masks, painful ass-heads that were a relief to get rid of – that's unfortunate, as this particular speech is difficult enough without any extra roadblocks. My solution may sound overly dramatic until you are reminded of the pressures involved in a theatrical production of this size, accompanied by the strictures of a very low budget.

The Moment

When Bottom wakes from his dream, like any good actor his first thought is for the play:

> When my cue comes, call me, and I will answer. My next is 'Most fair Pyramus'. Heigh-ho! Peter Quince? Flute, the bellows-mender? Snout, the tinker? Starveling? God's my life! Stolen hence and left me asleep!

The word 'asleep' casts him instantly back into his dream, or rather the feeling of his dream. I chose not to remember any of the precise details, only the sense of them and of the unutterable pleasure of so many secret dreams fulfilled. Does anyone not know this feeling – of trying to hang on to a really good dream? I am touching now on the actor's most difficult task: portraying something that is intimately familiar to everyone in the audience. I don't think there is any way an actor can communicate that kind of intimacy without honestly experiencing it then and there – the action of the character must be recognizable to each person in the auditorium and remind them of their own secret dreams, dreams they have forgotten. How else can an actor possibly achieve this without awakening such dreams within himself?

Of course, talking about it is easy. Doing it eight times a week is another story. Sometimes I would take too long waiting for inspiration, indulging in the 'moment' relishing that thoughtful, sad, desolate state. It's tempting to do that when you're alone onstage with a great speech, but what always saved me from myself was the finale of Bottom's Dream. It is the perfect ending to finish his dream the way it began: his last thought – the actor's thought – 'How can I use it?'

There is a story that Cocteau received a telegram informing him of his father's death, and that he screamed violently at the top of his lungs, but was immediately conscious of the need to record what he had just experienced to use for future reference.

'Man is but a patched fool if he will offer to say what methought I had'

You may find his energy wearing, but that is deliberate, because it sets up the one time he is stunned to silence, in 'Bottom's Dream'. When that happens, the silence is breathtaking. Suddenly, and possibly for the first time in his life, Bottom is speechless, as the feeling of his wonderful dream, the best dream ever, slowly vanishes. When he finally does speak, the words are common, nearly all of one syllable:

Shakespeare may have borrowed liberally from Corinthians (Old Testament) for this speech, but as usual, he made it his own: '... The eye of man hath not heard, the ear of man hath not seen, man's hand is not able to taste, his tongue to conceive, nor his heart to report, what my dream was ...'

Not one to mourn for long, Bottom just as suddenly comes back to himself with a plan to have the dream memorialized in poetry, to be spoken by him as part of the Interlude:

> ... I will get Peter Quince to write a ballad of this dream: it shall be called 'Bottom's Dream', because it hath no bottom; and I will sing it in the latter end of a play, before the Duke. Peradventure, to make it the more gracious, I shall sing it at her death.
> *Exit.*

The placement of this monologue, this quiet moment before the grand finale, was always a severe test for me. Self-indulgence was a very big seducer. I mean, here I was, alone onstage with this fabulous speech, coming out of an amazing dream, not wanting to let it go – everyone knows that feeling – and the temptation to milk it was almost overwhelming. To tell the truth, once in a while I did indulge, but believe me, not often.

All of the words in the 'Bottom's Dream' speech are simple and familiar; it's the nonsense in the middle of it that catches us off guard, that makes us smile, first *at* Bottom in anticipation of laughter, then *with* him as we realize, even as he does, that there are no words for an epiphany.

Act IV, scene ii

Quince, Flute, Snout and Starveling enter (Snug is absent);

they are lost without Bottom to play Pyramus. They speak of him as if at a memorial service.

FLUTE No, he hath simply the best wit of any handicraft man in Athens.
QUINCE Yea, and the best person too . . .

I believe that Bottom is loved. When the Mechanicals are faced with the possibility of performing without him they erupt with laments and paeans to his fine qualities. What a boost it was for Bottom to hear these endearments each night from a group of men who became closer with each rehearsal (and who have remained friends to this day, a rare thing in show business).

Richard Riehle played Peter Quince the carpenter, four-square builder of houses and plays, the author of the Interlude, 'Pyramus and Thisbe'. This taciturn actor, who was never without a book nearby, was an area of calm among us, and though he was physically imposing, his real power was intellectual no matter how loutish and simple the Mechanicals seemed. Richard as Quince left no doubt that, of these six working men, the carpenter was certainly capable of writing and directing a play. These aspects of his character were implied by his performance, although, in his exchanges with Bottom, additionally Quince was like a director/producer: he had to allow Bottom's flights of fancy to develop but also to bring him back to earth, and handle him well to ensure Bottom gave his best performance, without upsetting his ego or disturbing his pride. Shakespeare portrays him as the actor/manager to the artisans' company of players, keeping Bottom (and the others) more or less in line.

Joe Zaloom was Snout the tinker, and played the Wall in 'Pyramus and Thisbe'. Five foot eight, with a barrel chest and broad shoulders, he looked utterly dependable and as solid and reliable as any wall. When Joe says a thing, it is done, though his character has only a minimum of lines, which was pretty funny as he was probably the most outspoken member of the group, with a reputation as a political activist. There was a piece of business where Wall (Snout) was assaulted by Pyramus (Bottom) with a gentle slap on his face. At the first performance Joe showed up with a cigar in his mouth – a new addition. I saw the cigar, caught his eye and hesitated; he nodded slightly and I hit him. We kept that bit in for the duration, and little additions and surprises kept the show fresh and alive.

Joe Z. had the idea that, considering the success of the Mechanicals, we should convince Joe Papp to include us in all thirty-six productions of the NYSF's planned cycle; it was a brilliant concept, one that would have embraced the conditions Shakespeare worked under. Sadly, Mr Papp was not well and shortly thereafter we realized quite how bad he was. I am sure, if he'd lived, he would have found a way to feed this thread throughout his great series, displaying his own unit of players similar to how the Chamberlain's Men must have been, and introducing the American public to the concept of an American Shakespeare repertory company. What we Mechanicals learned as a unit remains our own discovery, and I have no doubt that, even though we haven't worked together since, we would still be completely in tune.

I should like to say a word about the term 'star' – the baggage is heady, and is a wrenching change from obscurity, but it has been attached to me and I am grateful for the opportunities and rewards it has brought to me and my family. The best thing about it is that I can work. Work, or rather the lack of it, is the actor's nightmare. And I am now able to work all the time.

The worst thing about fame is the loss of friendships. Many

cannot abide success. This group of Mechanicals let me know that not only was it OK for me to take the spotlight, it was my obligation. I had become prominent, and now, they seemed to say, I must prove myself worthy of that prominence, with the promise that they would stand firmly behind me. Thanks to them, I picked up my cue and ran with it. They gave me the impression that, without me, life would not be as good – yet when the wonderful actor Barton Haymen replaced me for a month, the show went on quite as well. I'd like to believe that it was not as strong without me but, truth to tell, I was proud of my dear friends for being craftsmen, artisans, actors first. I may have been terrific, but Shakespeare did fine with those seeds of a repertory company. No one is irreplaceable.

The Moment (II)

Something happened during Act IV that is still a mystery to me. I pride myself on being a highly professional actor, and this episode is out of character. Our production was such a hit that the run extended twice, and I took to wandering out front to watch the show from the vomitories. One night I became so involved watching the play as it moved along to a scene Bottom was supposed to be in that I remember thinking, 'Something's wrong up there, those guys are stalling . . . something's missing . . .' Well, those might not have been my thoughts exactly, but when I heard *my words being spoken by someone else*, I woke up and ran on to the stage from the auditorium. Was I asleep, or tired, or entranced with the beauty of the play? It doesn't matter, as there is no excuse for missing an entrance. I still don't know what happened. That play does transport one, so I'll blame it on Shakespeare.

Snug bursts on to say that the celebration is at hand. Bottom bursts on and tries to talk about what happened to him, but he can't, and finally tells the Mechanicals that their play is 'preferred'. They have been chosen as finalists in the Duke's festivities.

BOTTOM Not a word of me. All that I will tell you is, that the Duke hath dined. Get your apparel together, good strings to your beards, new ribbons to your pumps; meet presently at the palace; every man look o'er his part: for the short and the long is, our play is preferred. In any case, let Thisbe have clean linen; and let not him that plays the lion pare his nails, for they shall hang out for the lion's claws. And most dear actors, eat no onions nor garlic, for we are to utter sweet breath; and I do not doubt but to hear them say, it is a sweet comedy. No more words. Away! Go, away!'
Exeunt.

Act V

'But all the story of the night told over'

Act V is a stabilizing act, its purpose is to analyze all events that have preceded the happy nuptials and bring a conclusion to the play. We are restored to Athens (and perceived normality), at the point where we came in – the wedding arrangements of Theseus and Hippolyta are announced in the very first line of A Midsummer Night's Dream – 'Now, fair Hippolyta, our nuptial hour . . .' – and the ceremony is finally to take place.

HIPPOLYTA
'Tis strange, my Theseus, that these lovers speak of.
THESEUS
More strange than true. I never may believe

These antique fables, nor these fairy toys.
Lovers and madmen have such seething brains,
Such shaping fantasies, that apprehend
More than cool reason ever comprehends.
The lunatic, the lover, and the poet
Are of imagination all compact:
One sees more devils than vast hell can hold;
That is the madman: the lover, all as frantic,
Sees Helen's beauty in a brow of Egypt:
The poet's eye, in a fine frenzy rolling,
Doth glance from heaven to earth, from earth to heaven;
And as imagination bodies forth
The forms of things unknown, the poet's pen
Turns them to shapes, and gives to airy nothing
A local habitation and a name.
Such tricks hath strong imagination,
That if it would but apprehend some joy,
It comprehends some bringer of that joy:
Or, in the night, imagining some fear,
How easy is a bush suppos'd a bear!

HIPPOLYTA

But all the story of the night told over,
And all their minds transfigur'd so together,
More witnesseth than fancy's images,
And grows to something of great constancy;
But howsoever, strange and admirable.

Hippolyta and Theseus are discussing the dreams that have
been recounted by the young lovers, trying to understand
what these experiences were all about. Hippolyta naturally
takes the feminine view that these reported incidents are
interesting and strange and although they might not be able
to fully comprehend these events, the dreams must have pos-

itive meaning, for it seems as if it has ended well for all those involved. Theseus takes a masculine point of view, wary of this hokum, and forcing the voice of reason he gives a commentary comparing madness, love and art as three subjects that are beyond comprehension to the point of danger. I wonder if, through Theseus, Shakespeare is making a personal note about the burden of great art? – acknowledging the talent and skill of the artist, but also the elusive elements that lead to doubts and fears. Shakespeare's confessional, perhaps?

When Hippolyta and Theseus are joined by the newly married lovers – Lysander and Hermia; Demetrius and Helena – Theseus calls on his Master of the Revels, Philostrate, for the entertainments to fill the 'lazy time' between supper and sleep. (In our production, the role of Philostrate was absorbed by Egeus.) Philostrate gives Theseus a list and he reads this aloud and chooses 'Pyramus and Thisbe' to be performed, although Philostrate takes pains to point out that in his opinion it is a bad piece and he considers it amateurish.

THESEUS [*Reads.*]
'A tedious brief scene of young Pyramus
And his love Thisbe, very tragical mirth'?
Merry and tragical? Tedious and brief?
That is hot ice, and wondrous strange snow!
How shall we find the concord of this discord?

Again, I wonder if this is Shakespeare parodying all the times he had to argue with producers or backers about why something works in the theatre to a group of philistines? Having a go at them through the character of Theseus – who knows nothing of art – praising and influencing the play they are all to see whether it be a folly or not. In *Shakespeare in Love* Joe Fiennes, playing the Bard, was dealing with situations that we find familiar: writer's block, the search for a muse, material stolen from other playwrights – whatever it takes to make a fast buck; much like the theater and film world today – dominated by money, bums on seats. The film was highlighting Shakespeare's problems as those of a dramatist working to deadlines and juggling commissions as if he was already dealing with the contemporary dilemmas we all encounter of realizing a play or a film, though situated in Elizabethan England! It was a humorous way of doing it, but perhaps nothing has changed four hundred years later.

THESEUS
     I will hear that play;
  For never anything can be amiss
  When simpleness and duty tender it.

Theseus chooses 'Pyramus and Thisbe' for its seeming contradictions.

Quince duly mis-recites the Prologue, and the artisans enact the story of 'Pyramus and Thisbe' in dumb show. Their performance is punctuated by derisive comments from the audience, as the Interlude, written in archaic and comically inept rhyme, proceeds with banter back and forth between the players and the audience. Snout explains that he is playing the Wall through which Pyramus and Thisbe converse. Bottom as Pyramus and Flute as Thisbe arrange to meet at Ninus' tomb (an obvious connection to *Romeo and Juliet*). After Starveling (bearing a lantern), has finally explained that he represents the '*Man i' th' Moon*', Thisbe arrives and flees from Snug, the Lion, who worries her dropped mantle, which also reminds one of the tragedy that follows Desdemona's lost handkerchief in *Othello*. Pyramus finds the mantle, concludes that Thisbe has been eaten by the Lion, and kills himself. Thisbe returns, finds his body, and kills herself too. This could be more tongue-in-cheek playfulness from Shakespeare, illustrating that in drama you can do anything you want, but to do it successfully takes something else.

Tim Perez really came into his own with the opportunity of Thisbe's death, which comes after my spectacular death as Pyramus, and believe me, it was SPECTACULAR. Years earlier I had performed *The Fantasticks* in New York City, with a death scene that was based on Shakespeare's Bottom/ Pyramus, so I'd had some practice killing myself. As Pyramus, once was not enough for Bottom. I killed myself three times, rose from the dead, climbed up the side of a column, and somersaulted across the stage to end up on my knees with my arms wide begging for applause – which, of course, they had to give me, if for no other reason than fear of my doing even more! It was always a hit, but we were never prepared for Mighty Tim's Thisbe. When the clapping stopped, Tim entered, immensely tall in his gown, lace hat and bosoms, and took over with his own death scene. He was so quiet and so deeply touching that the audience seemed to hold their breath. He gently cradled me in his football-player arms, wept softly, then suddenly shrieked and started flinging me around like a rag doll. The audience erupted, they howled, they LOVED HIM. As Pyramus I was truly funny, but I turned out to be the warm-up. The success of the Mechanicals depends on the unit, and it was simply wonderful to be part of it. If one of us was neglected or glossed over, then the whole scene sagged.

It happened that in the death scene my continual experimenting got out of hand, and cost us one of our biggest laughs. One day, walking to work from my place in the Village, I spotted a child's plastic sword in the street. It was a hollow, two-foot-long, slightly damaged toy that I decided was perfect for Bottom's death. It was, and more. After stabbing myself and dying, Tim/Thisbe, raised the sword to kill him/herself, and as he did so, the sword sagged at the hilt, where it was broken. Well, it was a classic piece of slapstick and the audience howled. The end of the story is that in my attempt to improve the 'bit', I tried to stiffen the plastic blade slightly and broke the damn thing. I repaired it, but it was never the same; the scene was still fine, Tim was still great, but we never got that laugh back.

Once the Interlude is ended, Bottom offers an explanation to Theseus and suggests they could play an epilogue, or perhaps a dance. Theseus favors the dance and in declining the epilogue offers an alternative ending – close to the sort of suggestion a producer might think suitable to end a modern drama by almost completely forgetting the original concept. Once more, I think Shakespeare is having a laugh.

BOTTOM [*Starting up.*] No, I assure you; the wall is down that parted their fathers . . . Will it please you to see the epilogue, or to hear a Bergomask dance between two of our company?

THESEUS No epilogue, I pray you; for your play needs no excuse. Never excuse; for when the players are all dead, there need none to be blamed. Marry, if he that writ it had played Pyramus, and hanged himself in Thisbe's garter, it would have been a fine tragedy – and so it is, truly, and very notably discharged. But come, your Bergomask; let your epilogue alone.

Theseus declares it is past midnight and all must go to bed as it is almost fairy time.

Puck arrives followed by Oberon, Titania, and their train. They bless the house and the three married couples and ward off birth defects for their children. Left alone on stage, Puck speaks an epilogue, advising the audience to dismiss the play as a dream if they have not enjoyed it, but promising to improve if the audience applauds.

PUCK [*To the audience.*]

　　If we shadows have offended,
　　Think but this, and all is mended,
　　That you have but slumber'd here
　　While these visions did appear.
　　And this weak and idle theme,
　　No more yielding but a dream,
　　Gentles, do not reprehend:
　　If you pardon, we will mend.
　　And, as I am an honest Puck,
　　If we have unearned luck
　　Now to 'scape the serpent's tongue,
　　We will make amends ere long;
　　Else the Puck a liar call.
　　So, goodnight unto you all.
　　Give me your hands, if we be friends,
　　And Robin shall restore amends.
　　　　Exit.

PART III

A Midsummer Night's Dream:
Emergence of a Performance

Show of Shows

It is said that, in music, melody cannot be taught. You either have it or you don't. I believe that's also true of comedy. Sid Caesar's writers for the television series, *Show of Shows* included Neil Simon, Woody Allen, Carl Reiner and Mel Brooks, who have all spoken of shouting to be heard as they each tried to come up with the resolution to a skit or joke. Woody Allen, however, wasn't a shouter. Instead, he'd sit next to Carl Reiner, tell him his idea, and Reiner with his big voice would yell, 'Hey listen, Woody's got it!'

That group dynamic is common among entertainers, each finding his own way to be heard; but one person must assume leadership, and it had to be Bottom. If I had been playing any of the other Mechanicals, I would have completely supported whoever was our Bottom. My fellows allowed me that same respect. Although I was not always right, I always pushed, because there's only so much time to find some answers and, frankly, I was worried that a four-hundred-year-old joke wasn't funny any more. That may sound contradictory, as though we didn't trust the Master himself, but the reasons are simple: first, comics are naturally skeptical; and second, the 'Shakespearean clowns' we had seen, and continue to see, are not (in my opinion) funny; they're dreadful. Sure there are some obvious chuckles, but we weren't there for the chuckles. We were interested in screaming laughter. We hadn't the luxury of having worked together before, and didn't know each others' methods or habits. After charging recklessly into the scene and accomplishing six different directions, we started to go through the script very deliberately, trying any idea that came to mind. Trial-and-error is agonizing, but I don't know how else you can do comedy other than aloud, and we got pretty loud – like *Show of Shows* – and, like the lesson of Woody Allen, the quiet that followed the shouting was the most creative time. Since then I have worked with Allen on *Mighty Aphrodite*, and the calm on his movie set reflects the stillness out of which comes his trademark subtle humor.

Ultimately, in the course of a long run, many of our 'discoveries' were discarded. We'd drop two small laughs for one big one, which is one of the joys of an extended run – we became streamlined. After flailing around for a while, we'd stop for a frustrated breather, someone would make a suggestion – like, 'It's so dark we're scared to death in this jungle'; someone else wanted to make random animal noises, a third introduced food into the scene, another suggested that since we were probably beer drinkers we had to pee, but were too scared to go alone behind a tree and too macho to ask someone to go with us. The fun would seep back into us and we'd try again.

A. J. Antoon

A. J. Antoon enjoyed great triumphs with *Much Ado About Nothing*, *Measure for Measure* (Meryl Streep), *Taming of the Shrew* (Morgan Freeman and Tracey Ullman). The hallmarks of his work were originality and a talent for casting perfectly compatible players. The Mechanicals were primarily composites of Italian, Syrian, Scottish, Chicano, Irish, Welsh, German, Swedish and Dutch descent. The Fairy Kingdom had more exotic origins and all of color, from Puerto Rico, Cuba, Spain, Africa, South America and many parts of the Caribbean. In contrast the ruling class, the 'Colonialists', looked like an Ivy League reunion of prominent, privileged WASPs. This extraordinarily diverse bunch got along well enough and performed credibly enough to see our run extended twice; I repeat this because it's a phenomenon for a Shakespeare play in New York.

Sometimes tempers would flare and feelings got hurt, but with a director *in absentia* this was bound to happen to some extent. Yet had AJ been there all the time, I think we would have been inhibited. We rehearsed the three worlds separately in our respective groupings and consequently had AJ only for one third of the time. Actually what we were doing was finding out about each other, discovering how we all fit together; that became palpably clear one afternoon in the second week, when we sensed we were on to something – it was beginning to gel, so we called AJ in to take a look and shape it for us. He came in, we did it, and when he started to tell us how he thought we should do it, we knew immediately that he was dead wrong, and at that moment I believe we became a unit. We didn't have the 'answers', but we now felt we had the means to find them. The way AJ handled that situation is an example of his brilliance as a director, for he was confident enough to trust that we would develop something for him to work with, and that his own ego was not in question. It was funny to see his response; having asked him to come look at us, we almost immediately told him to go away.

When AJ concentrated he went into another dimension – his eyes would grow as round as saucers, his lips would part a little, and I swear you could feel him thinking – he was a passionate, highly intelligent, explosive man. There was no way to predict how he would respond to this treatment, in this instance our rejection of his ideas. If he had misinterpreted our intention, if he had felt his position threatened, it could have been a disaster. It's interesting how quiet it gets when someone really concentrates; we watched him think his way through to the best solution. In the end he gave us our heads! When he came out of his mini-trance, he said, 'OK. But you better have something to show me by tomorrow.' It was at this time that Tim Perez emerged as a brilliant comedian.

Big Tim

Up until that day, Big Tim, who played Flute, had been half-hearted in his choices, unsure of himself and his character. He had a tendency to mumble and I had difficulty hearing him. His timid approach could have been a result of focusing on the upcoming Thisbe (the lover he would be playing in the masque), but that was at the end of the play in Act V. Whatever the reason, he was sapping energy from the rest of us and I have very little patience with an actor who doesn't pick up on the life of the scene when we're all supposed to be participating. Everyone has a personal way of working, but we must all be 'on the same page'. The day that AJ delivered his ultimatum, we saw a dragon of a performance from Big Tim. It's not that Tim was responsible for the scene not working – we were all missing something – but when Tim made his breakthrough that day, it seemed to clarify things for the rest of us.

Timothy Perez, Francis Flute, is a Chicano, a handsome, six-foot-four college football player. Of course, as the biggest man in the company, he was to be Thisbe, sweetheart to my Pyramus. I didn't know at the time this was his first professional production, and I was pretty tough on him. If I had known, maybe I would have gone a little easier, but I don't think so. I became an impatient taskmaster with Tim, and my abruptness must have been intimidating to this young actor. My response to material is usually quick. If the idea doesn't feel right, I stop instantly and try something else. This can be disconcerting, I know, but when the discovery of a scene is at one's fingertips, the slightest hesitation might lose that moment, and there's no guarantee that you'll get it back. Tim and I were to be playing comic lovers, as reliant on one another as Abbot and Costello, but at this point, because of his anxiety, I didn't feel I could count on him. How wrong I turned out to be.

'If it ain't broke...'

There was a night when Richard was very sick (inevitably we all got sick from those tight quarters during the flu season) and was almost inaudible, so we decided to cut as many of his lines as possible and skip to the funny stuff at the end. We cut some of the repetitions, thinking it wouldn't make any difference – let me warn you about William Shakespeare: don't mess with him: the scene fell flat. Perhaps because of the changes, our timing was wrong and the rhythms were off, but as the saying goes, 'If it ain't broke, don't fix it.'

We didn't assign Richard's lines to anyone else because we had become arrogant in our success. We thought the play within a play was 'our little baby', so it wouldn't matter if we cut most of Peter Quince's lines – we'd just jump to the funny bits, the schtick, a little earlier than usual and nobody would be any the wiser. It simply didn't work. Shakespeare put Quince's lines in there because he needed every one of them. As for the 'bad' performances by the Mechanicals, there is nothing harder than performing 'being bad' successfully; you must do it sincerely, without 'winking' at the audience to let them know you're only kidding. It's hard to do well because the ego insists on a superior image. Try it. Try singing a familiar song slightly off key, as though you truly believe you are perfect. Being 'bad' is not good enough. It must be done artfully.

Character and characteristics

If I give the impression that *A Midsummer Night's Dream* is about someone named Bottom, I apologize; that's just the Bottom in me, trying to take over. There are few roles which challenge and excite; Bottom is one. It's ironic that, although historians acknowledge the freedom that Shakespeare's clowns enjoyed, they cringe at the prospect of an unanticipated aside from a contemporary actor, particularly a contemporary American actor. However, we should ask ourselves what we expect from the theater. Personally, I expect inspiration, both as a performer and as a member of the audience. The main problem with that expectation is the high percentage of disappointment. Still, isn't a failed attempt at inspiration more interesting than no attempt at all? Bottom would certainly think so. His need for expression captivates me. He never monitors himself. His freedom is buoyant and irrepressible, percolating right at the end of his tongue.

No one else could have spoken so freely, or behaved so naturally, within each distinct society. Puck deals with all three worlds too, but as the meddlesome goblin he is perhaps the dark side of Bottom, I think, and much of the time he manipulates people rather than engaging with them, primarily serving his master, Oberon. He's fun but malicious, and irresponsibly selfish. Bottom appears to be selfish but he sincerely wants what is best for the entire community, for everyone. Where could Bottom not fit in, if only for a little while? When the Fairy Queen invites him to be her lover, it's the most natural thing in the world, as is talking to a cobweb, a peaseblossom, and a moth. When he is performing the tragedy of

Pyramus and Thisbe, the court's derisive comments roll off his back and he boldly offers the Duke the chance to see the Mechanicals do an additional 'number' – epilogue or Bergomask.

Even as I write, the memory of the experience more than fifteen years ago pulls me into Bottom's frame of mind, and my reflections are colored by his personality, which is what usually happens when actors feel their work has been a success. On the first day of rehearsal it's easy to anticipate and project a mixture of actor and role. In the playing of a character these two elements get confused and overlap, because the process of becoming a character begins long before that day. The process begins as soon as an actor reads a script, subconsciously selecting characteristics that might be suitable for the role. I suppose it's like the early stage of pregnancy: it might not show, but it's part of everything you do, gestating and nurturing, even while you sleep. Though aware of all this, I still found myself at the first occasion we were all together marveling at the terrific casting. 'How right they are for their parts.'

When we had overcome our problems and the Mechanicals really were a unit, we'd only tackled the first hurdle. The next stage was to integrate our group with the play and come together successfully with the rest of the company.

A glance let you know instantly who was who – a very important element in this play of separate worlds. There was no doubt that the largish, rough-looking men were the Mechanicals; the sexy, exotic dancers were Fairy Folk; and the elegant whites, Athenians. Watching them even slightly behave as their characters at this first reading revealed much about their preconceptions, which were bound to change, but nevertheless were surfacing. The tilt of a head, crossing of a leg, a certain kind of laughter – all that was not merely nerves;

it was also subtle practicing. The fact is, of course, that they too had already begun a subtle metamorphosis. Some actors insist on discovering the character only during rehearsals, and avoid working on the text until then. They believe this method avoids locking them into patterns, or pursuing an interpretation that may be disconnected from the rest of the cast. Despite all that, especially with a classical role, I don't think it's possible to ignore the character in such a complete way, as a certain familiarity with the role (and the play) already exists. Especially if you are about to perform it. So rather than squander my energy pretending not to think about 'elephants', I usually come to rehearsal prepared, lines memorized. My teacher, Uta Hagan, would throttle me for doing it, but I have found that this is best for me. I enjoy the freedom of not having to search for the words, and as my 'interpretations' are never etched in stone, they are malleable. Nevertheless I make a show of holding the script for a couple of weeks for the sake of peace within the company.

Preparation

The advantage of knowing the lines from the outset goes beyond the simple freedom from the book, as the function of reading aloud is very different from reciting from memory. When you read, your eye dictates what you say. When you recite, as you search for words or phrases, your imagination ranges and selects, sometimes supplying alternative words or phrases – what you come up with is never as good as Shakespeare, but improvising in blank verse is good exercise that increases one's confidence with the language. The disadvantages are rigidity and insularity. When I played King Lear at Cambridge for Robert Brustein, it was a great success, and it too was extended beyond its initial run. However, when it transferred to New York some years later (to the same theatre where I did Bottom), I gave the same performance in this 280-seat house that I had given in the 2,000-seater. The director and designer were also the same, but it was a new cast, and I didn't re-think the role, or make allowances. I simply did what had worked before, and it was a critical disaster. The notices were terrible, really terrible. I'd like to have another chance with Lear, and this time I won't come to the first rehearsal 'memorized'. Mostly. Because Lear never leaves you; like any of the great roles, he takes you over when you least expect it, and the lines come rushing back and you long to do it just once more.

Holding such strong feelings about preparation, I was pleased to see that so many others had done some homework. Even at the first rehearsal I could see where certain actors were headed, clearly with some firm ideas about what they wanted to do and outlining a foundation to build upon. Interestingly, Katharine Hepburn and Spencer Tracy made nine movies together, one of the most successful acting partnerships; yet their attitudes to preparation were polar opposites: Katharine Hepburn worked thoroughly over every detail of a script for weeks ahead of filming, whereas Spencer Tracy would, at best, casually glance at it before first day of shooting. The outcome can be seen in their different styles, both equally valid.

There's a telling incident from that first day in the studio. Titania was played by Lorraine Toussaint, a sexy, no-nonsense actress with fire in her blood, who seemed related, in temperament at least, to the great Haitian revolutionary Toussaint. Her relationship with the handsome, powerful actor Carl Lumbly (Oberon), was such a mirror image of the one that exists between their characters in the play that I found myself staring at them as they argued over where to sit. Carl/King

Oberon wanted her on his right, where he thought a Queen 'belongs', whereas Lorraine/Titania preferred to be surrounded by her cast of handmaidens. I thought it was an improvisation they had conspired on, but no, they really meant it. What fun it was to see the Fairies enjoying this little tussle, standing in attendance, waiting for their future King and Queen to make a decision. When it was settled, all of the Fairy Folk sat down together, except for Puck, played by Geoffrey Owens. At the time he was starring in the television series *The Bill Cosby Show* and frequently needed to leave early to tape the show. He didn't want to be disruptive at his early exit and so sat slightly apart, which gave him freedom to move around while the rest of the cast were sitting in our chairs. This typified Puck's elfish superiority to us earthbound mortals. In an instant he would lean in from one to another of us, giving the impression that he was everywhere among us.

It was delightful and funny, but the reason he could do it so effectively in rehearsals was that we were all sitting close to each other. Spread across the stage it would prove much harder to accomplish, because he has to appear (magically) in several places (almost) at once. Agile as Geoffrey was (and later his replacement, John Leguiziamo), the scene depends on the audience's indulgence – again, Coleridge's 'willing suspension of disbelief' – because it's physically impossible without some kind of theatrical mirrors, which we couldn't afford. Incidentally, some years later I saw the problem solved in *A Dream In Hanoi*, a documentary film I narrated about the making of *A Midsummer Night's Dream* (which was the first theatrical co-production between Vietnam and the United States): the Vietnamese co-director insisted on six silent assistants for Puck and it worked brilliantly.

The presence of several strong-willed actors in one company can obviously be touchy. Fortunately with three distinct groups, rehearsing independently partially solved the problem of too many leaders in one room. Paradoxically it might have set off a number of mini-dramas in the newly created micro-societies until a natural order emerged and allegiances formed within each group, and resettled with loyalties that would shape and distinguish them. We benefited further by this arrangement, as it effectively tripled the rehearsal time, as we were not waiting for others to finish and therefore could work all day. AJ circulated between the separate rehearsal rooms and would join us periodically for a few hours to look at our progress, direct or redirect us, and then leave us alone to work further by ourselves. It was a remarkable show of trust on his part, and it seems to have been a good plan. My only regret concerning this rehearsal schedule was that, except for my dear Mechanicals, I didn't get a chance to see the other actors as they grew and changed. I enjoy the process and it is rewarding to watch good actors work on their character and evolve a role; but we weren't effectively together until the first dress rehearsal shortly before opening night.

First read-through

The first read-through is usually a rambling, dry, almost inaudible affair, but there was nothing tentative about my approach – it was an all-out attack. When I attack a text early on, I am challenging the others to be bold, to take a chance right now, at this moment, among colleagues. We should be able to trust one another. If I am willing to step up and fall on my face, then why can't they too? What is there to lose? In this way I break the ice for anyone willing to jump in with me. No one has to jump, but at least they have the choice.

The main problem I foresaw with the preparation of the role was committing myself to Bottom's freedom while maintaining some sense of discipline – a kind of managed anarchy. My choice was to play Bottom full-out – but there's so much of him in me that I didn't know where to start. I decided to just jump in and see what came out. The idea of a character in a play functioning independently of the actor performing him may be confusing, but hasn't it happened to you when you put on a costume or mask, or more likely, found yourself in an unusual situation where you had to push yourself forward? Doesn't someone else, someone quite different, subtly come alive within you?

Ralph Richardson

My plan was to have no plan: I leapt right in and, of all things, what came out was an English accent. This was quite a shock, but I wanted to let it take its course and listen to it for a while, to find out where it was coming from. It wasn't long before I realized I was doing one of my favorite actors, Ralph Richardson. American actors have shaped most of my work, from stories of Edwin Booth to the recordings and films of John Barrymore to the genius of Marlon Brando, but British actors have had a considerable influence too, especially John Gielgud, Laurence Olivier and Richardson. They feel like an essential part of my long-distance apprenticeship; but Ralph Richardson was always closest to my heart. I wish I could have seen him play Bottom, but then I probably would have stolen all his stuff. There are stories about him forgetting his lines and substituting any other Shakespeare part that came to mind – perhaps this is just part of the folklore that surrounds great actors (the anecdotal idiosyncrasies, etc.), and maybe the story is exaggerated; but it feels right and suits Bottom, don't you think? I have seen him perform several times, and he gave the impression that he didn't know what was going to come out of his mouth next, but nevertheless with the reassurance that everything would be fine. It was as if he were inventing the words as he went along. What astounding courage that takes, because it requires sublime technique to appear not to have 'learned' the words and then convince yourself it's true. The danger is that you can forget things, like cues and entrances. It demands a serene faith in oneself, faith that the correct line will be there. I do not believe it was forgetfulness but conscious technique (although I also like to encourage these legendary stories). His work is too consistent to be an accident. When I've asked his colleagues about him the initial response has invariably been – a smile. I sense a comradeship that reaches beyond his apparent solitariness. If I may use a term that is overused (but I believe accurate in this case), British actors loved and cherished him, whilst Olivier – though greatly respected and admired – was (perhaps) not regarded with such affection. So even if the accent was definitely out, Ralph was to be part of my characterization.

With this seemingly haphazard approach I took my lead from the great Edith Evans, who showed up at a rehearsal with all kinds of baubles and props and costume pieces, and used them all. When the director finally asked what she was doing, she replied, '*Everything*, with the hope of finding *something*.' The first day of *A Midsummer Night's Dream* was much like that for the whole company.

All actors complain of short rehearsal periods, as so much is thrown at us to absorb: the concept, the music, the design, the choreography – everything. No one likes to work this way, although our objections were tempered by sensing the importance of our production as the initial offering in Joe Papp's proposed six-year marathon of all Shakespeare's plays. Our play would be pivotal, but it would also be examined under a microscope.

Is it every acting company's conceit that if Shakespeare saw the best of their work he would be delighted? This hypothesis is not as far-fetched as it sounds. If audiences cheer at the end of a show, of course the playwright would be pleased. Or would he? Some years ago there was a highly acclaimed modern production of *A Midsummer Night's Dream*, audiences were shouting bravo almost before the final curtain, but I really disliked that production, where there was so much clever direction that I lost track of the language. I also hated the short shrift given the Mechanicals – they simply weren't funny. Every production has to make decisions about the balance of comedy and drama and specifically the function of comedy to counterpoint the 'serious' themes of the play. Our interpretation was to make the Mechanicals crucial and my belief is that Shakespeare also saw it that way. Other directors and other productions make different decisions. Shakespeare would no doubt have been pleased about the action at the box office and the huge interest it generated, along with the director's refusal to be bound by tradition – but would he have liked it? That was the question I asked myself about our production. I know the actors and dancers had great affection for it. In forty years in the theater I've never known so many performers arrive at the theater so early. They'd drift in hours before curtain and just hang out, wanting to be together. This is worth noting, wouldn't you say – people arriving for work hours early? Not only did we like each other, but collectively we must have known this was a unique experience and should be relished as much as possible, since it probably wouldn't happen again for a long time.

Shaping Bottom

All the variable signs that indicate the potential strengths of the performance were good: terrific role; talented director; great producer and lovely company – how could I miss? Simple – by letting Bottom take over. Like most actors, I begin to assume the qualities of the character. If the character is allowed free rein, a sort of uncensored coursing, he'll lead you to places that only the unconscious can reveal. But you must trust your impulses, and that's the hardest part, because when they're off, you risk looking like a fool.

Bottom couldn't wait to get to the theater, pulling me out of bed full of ideas for the performance that night. He reminded me of what Geraldine Page used to say of matinées: 'Today we get to do it twice.' I had to keep telling him that he wasn't the whole play, only part of it. He told me that he was much more than I gave him credit for, and he was right. Bottom's presence is felt throughout the play, even when he is not onstage. His connection to it is ours, and he is the only character who experiences a profound revelation, the only one aware, however briefly, of the deep mystery of his life. He was also trying to heal the wound I was suffering. I must have been limping from the *Frankie and Johnny* episode, unwilling to commit myself fully to the dominant role that Bottom plays, for fear of once again being 'shot down'. I take great pride in being an actor, and believe in the relevance of my work, but at that point, I was unsure of anything. It was a great coming-together of actor and character when finally I accepted that the reason I couldn't recognize Bottom's prominence was the faded confidence in my own. It was like surfacing to take a deep breath. I agreed with Bottom that, yes, he was a dominant presence in the entire play, and I had some value too! He was the thread to the separate worlds, and it was his, and my, responsibility to behave accordingly.

In the early stages of rehearsal Bottom was excessively energetic, even for Bottom, and I realize now that he must have been compensating for my own personal lethargy. He pried me away from my self-pity. What a relief it was to become involved in my life in the play. It is my nature to look after the welfare of the company, partly because of my relative prominence and outspoken defense of actors. I generally function as the Equity Deputy – a sort of ombudsman, or actor's representative. I take the idea of leadership seriously, and am usually the first to arrive at the theater and the last to leave. In that sense I suppose I permeated the backstage area just as Bottom did the stage.

In order to maintain some perspective I decided to read the script each day before rehearsal. The discipline required to do this every morning is a rigid one, and can backfire on you. At first I found myself playing all the roles, but gradually the other characters began to assert themselves, and I started to exert some control over Bottom in response. There is a tendency to concentrate only on the page in front of you rather than on the wider world of the play and react by complaining of the scarcity in your character's lines, at least if you're Bottom.

Thinking as the character thinks

Thinking as the character thinks is the first connection and it usually happens much later in rehearsals. The process of building a character has been examined in very precise detail (frequently tedious) by too many actors and, along with many directors, they ungenerously save all the credit for themselves. Shame on them. The character must be acknowledged, for without it, the rest doesn't matter. I'll try to describe what I mean but admit it is hard to do without sounding mystical, or pretentious – though Bottom is especially helpful, as I believe he clearly illustrates our understanding of the essential difference between the American and the British approach to acting. This contrast is blurring with the exchange of prominent directors and actors, but personally I think the difference is healthy, and I hope the two approaches remain distinct.

It's possibly an apocryphal story but this is the way I heard it: Olivier was so inspired that actors and crew were drawn to the wings, a truly extraordinary performance, something which, as great as he was, they had never seen before. Curtain comes down, he hurries to his dressing room. A fellow actor finds him slumped in a chair, sobbing. The actor asks him if he knows what he's just accomplished, and Olivier says he does. So why is he in tears? Olivier replies, 'Because I don't know how I did it.'

The details may not be accurate but, clearly, control is uppermost in his mind. He was upset because he knew he couldn't repeat that inspirational performance at will; it came from a place outside his comprehension. His search for consistency is admirable, yet it does epitomize the difference I spoke of between British and American. For Olivier, craft was an end, the goal to transport the audience, not himself. The American actor wants to transport both the audience and himself, and considers craft the means by which to do it. Unfortunately the average American actor skips the 'craft' part, resulting in the kind of lazy self-indulgence that invites anyone at all to try their hand at acting. No wonder there is such contempt for American actors – that is, until they become famous.

Bottom pretends to be in control, most of the time, but you're never quite sure what he *might* do next, and this combination of polished craft and explosive improvisation enables him to communicate comfortably with both the ultra-civilized Duke of Athens and the wild Queen of the Fairies, who is spellbound (but Bottom is unaware of this).

I believe in control, up to a point. Once I discover a phrase or piece of business, I can perform it pretty consistently, yet not slavishly. Preparation, which is grounded in technique, is necessary, but people don't come to the theater to watch you parade your technique. The majority of the audience isn't sufficiently aware of technical details to observe them in your performance, although without the specifics they might be aware of something missing. Preparation doesn't mean a thing if you're not willing to leave it all in the wings the moment you step onto the stage and trust that your character will come alive. I never doubted that Bottom would live – so the task became a kind of game between him and me: how much freedom I would allow him, and how much he would chide me for my meekness.

This internal battle is not uncommon. In order to achieve a living representation of life, the actor must believe in the importance of the character he is portraying. With the information available to him, he creates a world outside the play, one in which he is the star, sometimes going so far as to imagine, in fine detail, what brought him to his entrance – thus the battle between the huge central role he has created for himself outside the script, and the actuality of 'I cannot pull a cart nor eat dry oats, but if it be man's work, I'll do't' – *King Lear*.

You can see evidence of this in old black-and-white films when a fine character actress has only three lines, yet there is a history to her character, as well as a future. Those same three lines spoken in a film today have less to do with acting than behavior, and the behavior is usually: '*Look at me, look at me, look at me*'; they throw the scene out of balance because they don't think of the play as a whole, only of their part in it. With these actors there is never a battle. They know the play is about them, and everyone else be damned. They are to be avoided at all costs.

During a rehearsal there is a sort of observing third eye that monitors what is being done. It then selects and records the successful attempts for future reference. The 'safe' actor continues to monitor himself in performance, never taking his eyes off himself. He preens and struts, confident in his ability to repeat a practiced phrase (with no surprises); he could do it in his sleep.

A performance has nothing to do with watching oneself. Standing in the wings waiting for an entrance should be like preparing to step off into space: you've no idea what will happen. I don't want to give the impression that it's some kind of mystical journey – you must have wit and craft enough to support you when something goes wrong. The artist must be aware of the world he is part of, yet not completely controlling; he must be open to whatever possibility. The work continues to evolve, particularly with an audience in front of you; the creative process is one of the reasons they have come to the theater. Where else can they actually watch an artist creating something? That will never happen if the actor plays it safe. Some actors don't take chances and are very good at what they do, with a dazzling, commendable technique. But finally, they are just too scared to take that chance.

What kept this give-and-take under control was ultimately the outcome: The Performance. Bottom was to be allowed considerable freedom, but there would come a time to make decisions. In rehearsals you can whimsically switch from Brooklyn street theater to British music hall, but not in performance. The preparation of a play has a particular technique that is quite distinct from performance technique, and you can always spot an actor who doesn't make that distinction. He's the one who doesn't really need an audience because, no matter what happens, his performance is never going to vary. I'm not talking about taking liberties with the script; I'm talking about including the audience so that they feel an intimate part of the process, and a belief they'll understand every word of this old play. The only way I know to accomplish this is to make the words my own by connecting my life and imagination to these words. AJ made this connection easier by relocating ancient Athens into balls-out Bahia, Brazil, during the colonization of South America (late nineteenth/early twentieth century). This concept 'Americanized' the play, and relieved us a little of the anxiety that so many on this side of the Atlantic experience when we do Shakespeare. AJ had successfully 'relocated' the setting of several other plays, and the ease with which his actors fulfilled their roles is attributable partly to the setting – familiar rather than alien.

How do I bring the everyday world that I live in and what's important to me in that world into my characterization of Bottom without warping the play or ignoring a responsibility to my fellow actors? By trusting the words completely. This is more difficult than it sounds. Shakespeare comes with so much baggage that reading the play has become a burden of responsibility rather than a liberating pleasure; with the different rhythms of speech and the odd language, for many it's like learning to read all over again. Russian and German actors tell me that Shakespeare is much more accessible to them and to their audiences because they don't have so many explanatory textual footnotes, for the simple reason that translations of the text are relatively free of archaic terms. Another handicap is the burden of scholarship that smothers some actors and overshadows the reason the play was written: to be performed. Scholarship is essential to the actor only in so much as it serves the performance. I am not onstage to display my research. I am here to act, to do, to communicate.

My task is to understand the words intimately and speak them so that the audience instantly grasps my meaning. The resonance of the material should take place after, never during, a performance. It should remain subconscious, surfacing involuntarily, as in *Oedipus Rex* when the audience is suddenly overwhelmed with the impulse to warn Oedipus against his fate; that can only happen if the play carries you along with it and rivets your attention on the characters and story. If philosophic considerations become a primary concern, it's a sign that the actors have lost the audience; immediacy is the soul of the theater and without the active participation of everyone involved we simply go through the motions of watching and listening. Too many actors mouth the words as though they are conscious of fulfilling an obligation to a dead myth rather than to a living genius. *Shakespeare in Love* brought Shakespeare-the-man to life, and Baz Luhrmann's modern interpretation of *Romeo and Juliet* proved how popular this work could be if we think about presentation. Those young actors appear comfortable with him, but while the actor tries to invest his whole self in the performance, it's a little tough when you're using words that no longer fadge, that don't mesh, that are illogical, either to you or your audience, although an astonishing number of Shakespeare's speeches speak directly to us and our condition. For example, the wretchedness of Lear required very little research in preparation, for as I walked to work each night I could see the homeless in the streets around me and hear the words:

Poor naked wretches, wheresoe'er you are,
That bide the pelting of this pitiless storm,
How shall your houseless heads and unfed sides
Your loop'd and window'd raggedness, defend you
From seasons such as these? Oh, I have ta'en
Too little care of this!
     (*King Lear*, Act III, scene iv)

Bottom's final monologue has much broader implications. When he realizes that it is impossible to describe what he's been through, he speaks to those of us who stood on the streets of New York and saw the Twin Towers fall on September 11th: 'The eye of man hath not heard, the ear of man hath not seen, man's hand is not able to taste . . . nor his heart to report, what my dream was.'

Again, all that the actor needs to do for inspiration is look around him.

A formidable mirror

If I seem to be flogging this theme, it's because I take him literally when William Shakespeare calls actors 'the abstract brief chronicle of the time'. He is relying on Bottom to abstract Our Own Time. When Snow White's stepmother smashes the magic mirror for telling the truth, we understand how she feels; anyone who has ever really looked into a mirror understands, and Bottom is a formidable mirror. He reflects everything we feel, he hides nothing and projects everything, and this makes him dangerous, not only to himself, but to those around him, as there are some truths about ourselves we would rather not see exposed. His weaknesses are ours, his ignorance too.

Bottom represents the reason a play must be performed – so that it will be fully realized. In the first place, that's why it was written and in the second, I believe that Shakespeare is counting on actors to bring his words to life in a direct, comprehensible way to a contemporary, general audience. I think he knew this would keep his work fresh. Even the minor plays should be performed regularly – let the public decide for themselves why one play is better than another. There are some truths that simply cannot be discovered other than collectively, in performance, and suggestions that Shakespeare's plays should only be read aloud are hogwash. Professor Harold Bloom, a leading proponent of that conceit, complains, 'I am so weary of badly directed Shakespeare that I would prefer to attend public readings rather than performances of the plays.' I agree with him on so much, but here we part company.

Is he unaware that failures are necessary in any performance – especially the accomplishment of a great performance – and that without failures there are no triumphs? Actors cannot repair their mistakes in private. We have to do it in public, right there in front of an audience, because the truth, subjective though it may be, can't be discovered in rehearsal, and then trotted out for each performance. It must be discovered each night. Every time you step on to the stage it's an undiscovered world, because it's a different audience, with a new energy and expectation. There are always variables, it is not a reading in isolation and under control, and with each performance we need to make a new connection. I'm aware that Bloom is speaking for himself (and we are all entitled to a non-proprietary opinion), but Shakespeare didn't write his plays as intellectual exercise. He wrote them to be performed, by actors, in a theatre, before an audience.

Shakespeare loved actors and admired their power, their delight, and their necessary role in catharsis. Bottom takes us on several journeys with him, but no matter where he goes, Bottom should project the image of a man in complete accord with his world, someone who is precisely where he should be at all times. Thus he becomes the center of any universe, something every one of us is capable of being.

William Shakespeare is counting on Bottom's honesty to keep his writing alive and immediate. Bottom may exaggerate, but he doesn't lie. His connection with the audience is comfortable, encouraging him to step over the established boundaries, to enjoy the play along with them. His only requirement is to tell the truth. The audience in New York City changed considerably after September 11th – looking for new meanings in familiar lines – a commonality, or a center around which to rally in order to find some relevance in this chaos. Shakespeare supplies a glimpse of this in Bottom's great 'The eye of man hath not heard' speech. He seems to be saying there is no logic or rationale to this life – there is only incomprehensibility, acceptance and, finally, hope. Bottom is the touchstone, the alembic through which these revelations are made.

The comedy has a dark undercurrent, a persistent reminder that love is not easy, it must be won, and once won, cared for. 'The course of true love never did run smooth.' All the lovers in this play learn this lesson, but only by the light of the moon, the ultimate romantic image. Moonlight. Even in print it's evocative. To say it, is to feel it: moonlight, *la luna*, lunacy, loony. If I ever do it again there'll be a moon at each rehearsal, even if it is just a picture pinned to the wall.

The value of a proper atmosphere from the very beginning is extremely important to me, and from the second day of rehearsal I began wearing my version of the costume. AJ set our production in South America, and as I am from the border of Mexico, with working-class origins, I felt I had a very good idea of how a laborer from South America would dress: a beat-up, busted straw hat; bare feet in old sandals; ragged cotton trousers tied with rope; a faded shirt open to the waist; with a worn, raveled kerchief tied round my neck. I felt rakish, free, and a little bit dangerous. Where does Bottom get his confidence? I think it's rooted in his imagination. After all, he's a working stiff with no future, so what else does he have? The longer I worked on the role, the more certain I became that

Bottom, a weaver, has never woven a thing. I'd imagine him at his place of work with some wool or flax in his hands, always on the verge of weaving, only to remember some rare bit of poetry, or observation that needed expounding. The working class in South America is full of the vivacious imagination that perfectly fits this play.

Considering the dangerous times he was living in, that's rather unhealthy. The violent suppression of the lower classes is still a part of our lives, and not only in the Third World. Bear in mind the situation: a noble's wedding, but with the undercurrent of political union.

At the beginning of the play Theseus says:

Stir up the Athenian youth to merriments;
Awake the pert and nimble spirit of mirth;
Turn melancholy forth to funerals;
The pale companion is not for our pomp.
Hippolyta, I woo'd thee with my sword,
And won thy love doing thee injuries;
But I will wed thee in another key,
With pomp, with triumph, and with revelling.

Ameliorating words in a wounded time; but you can bet there's an armed guard just out of sight. By contrast, in the Fairy world Oberon's disagreement with Titania caused by a dispute over a favorite child is resolved with a bawdy invention (her digression with Bottom) by the great Fairy King. It is a peaceful solution that spares the child and saves their love, and a stark contrast to the parallel human world that resolves its differences by violently sacrificing both children and love. Puck is still right: we're a bunch of fools.

However, with Bottom that's not an insult, he would have been a great fool, in the greatest tradition.

A Bottom for Our Time

What a brilliant concept the Fool is! It's a post that should be part of every government; he surely could have saved the United States a lot of embarrassment. But since one of Bottom's most endearing qualities is his innocence, I'm afraid that were he exposed to politics for a while, the innocence would vanish, and with it some of what he floats on, the thing that sets him apart and sustains him – his imagination. It's also the thing that makes him dangerous. A good fool is a mirror to his king, and I don't think Theseus would have put up with Bottom. I believe that when the Mechanicals perform before the court, the royal guard is keeping a sharp eye on this rabble, especially the one with the big mouth. And they're right.

The Fool is worth exploring for his social commentary and the dangers of shattering taboos, challenging orthodoxy and making people examine themselves, which sounds to me much like the role of the actor. The American authorities particularly find this individual disturbing. You will find Bottom's twentieth-century incarnation in various roles and characters from the world of entertainment – for instance, in Peter Barnes's play *Clap Hands, Here Comes Charlie*; but as Charlie, Bottom has lost some innocence and grown some claws.

The comedian Lenny Bruce was a Bottom who changed America's perception of words with his revolutionary idea that there was no such thing as 'foul language' and it made him an icon for the emerging counter-culture, earning him a good living for years. The law tried to curtail him with malicious prosecutions for obscenity and drug busts, which all chipped away at his sanity. He also made sport of President Kennedy's assassination. He spent the remainder of his life in and out of courts fighting 'freedom of speech' battles. Victimized and depressed, he died from a drug overdose. It's still dangerous to insult the king.

Peter Sellers, perhaps the most assimilated of modern-day clowns, in both his life and his work, was a poignant Chauncey Gardner in *Being There* (Hal Ashby's film of Jerzy Kosinski's novel), a simple man elevated to the Presidency, at first seen as a fool but then regarded as sage and savior whose banal statements are taken for wisdom by an electorate craving enlightened leadership. A contrast with his Cold War President (with a council of fools) in Stanley Kubrick's *Dr Strangelove*.

Bill Maher was the daring and witty host of *Politically Incorrect*, a pretty outrageous show that was outspoken in both its content and its language – refreshing and popular, especially the no-holds-barred attacks on national politicians. But the comment that did him in was a rejoinder to a statement that the men who crashed into the Twin Towers were cowards. Maher said that it was a horrible thing they had done, but they couldn't be called cowards, inasmuch as they gave their lives for their beliefs. The cowards, he said, are those who sit in the safety of some bunker sending rockets hundreds of miles away. Free speech be damned; he lost his show in a flash.

The two most prominent humorists who were politically inclined were Will Rogers and Bob Hope. Rogers targeted both political parties mercilessly. Hope was more a cheerleader for the Republicans, going so far as to share his gag writers with Nixon and Spiro Agnew. Of the two, I think Will Rogers was a great fool in the classic sense, and would not have hesitated to throw pies at anyone who came up with a stupid idea.

The Fool is the smartest character in *King Lear*. He is absent when Lear disowns Cordelia because had he been present he would have devised a way to prevent the tragedy that took place.

Truth is the touchstone

Whatever the play, truth is always the touchstone, and needs constant re-examining. I come to the theater to be someone else and you come to the theater to believe me. How successful I am at convincing you – and myself – of the reality of the play depends on my connection with the words. I'm not about to describe Shakespeare's language beyond how it affects me. Preparing Salieri, I listened to several excerpts of Mozart, literally hundreds of times, and the music continually surprised me with its invention and its sheer beauty. That's how I feel about playing Shakespeare: like a musician playing Mozart, privileged, challenged, complete. But no matter how sophisticated, intricate and beautiful the language, the effect is, essentially, primitive. Apart from cosmetic alterations the theater is as recognizable today as fifty thousand years ago – we wear animal skins, bits of rock and metal; we pierce our bodies and gather in cave-like spaces lit by artificial means; sometimes we use fire and water. Personally, I like that sense of continuity.

Does it sound like I enjoyed doing this play? I did. It remains the favorite of my forty-year career. There have been other performances that earned me higher praise, and higher salaries, but none that spoke so intimately to what I need and love in the theater: community. I have never doubted my work since, and there is no question that Shakespeare is responsible, because the returns on that experience (so long ago) have never stopped, the lines remain fresh and the memory dear. This may be true of other playwrights, but not on the same scale.

At the New York Public Theater (officially off-Broadway) we were a big hit: interviews, celebrities dropping by backstage, invitations to events – the works. A gambling casino sent a huge limousine to pick us up after the show to take us to Atlantic City, for a night in an opulent suite with a view of the ocean and everything on the house. We piled into the limo after the show and at the casino no one objected or was put out by the way we were dressed. Shakespeare was welcome everywhere.

There is a kinship among actors who have played the same roles, and I would like to believe that, sitting around with a bunch of Bottoms from the various parallel worlds, we would have a fine old time comparing notes, discussing problems, acting out our triumphs, trying to top each other in the death scene! And I am sure that while each of us would bow to Will Kempe, the possible originator, we would at the same time know that the only Bottom for us is our own. For as much as Shakespeare may have loved Kempe, he loved each of us just as well, because, irrational as it sounds, he makes an actor feel as though he wrote the part specifically for him.

It's very hard to explain what is so deeply personal.

I could act it for you.